# A Republic,
# If You Can Keep It

# A REPUBLIC, IF YOU CAN KEEP IT

## by Earl Warren

QUADRANGLE BOOKS

A NEW YORK TIMES COMPANY

Library of Congress Catalog Card Number: 76–162804

FIRST EDITION

BOOK DESIGN BY WARREN CHAPPELL

EAGLE DEVICE: WOODCUT BY FRITZ KREDEL

*To one of the
most important segments
of our citizenry,
the millions of American mothers—
including my wife, NINA—
whose fondest hope is
that their children will be
responsible citizens,
and whose faith in humanity
and love of freedom
sustain their belief
that this will be achieved.*

As the delegates of the Constitutional Convention trudged out of Independence Hall on September 17, 1787, an anxious woman in the crowd waiting at the entrance inquired of Benjamin Franklin, "Well, Doctor, what have we got, a republic or a monarchy?"

"A republic," Franklin replied, "if you can keep it."

From Notes of Dr. James McHenry, *one of the delegates to the Federal Convention of 1787 and a signer of the draft of the Constitution.* (*Adapted from* Documents Illustrative of the Formation of the Union of the American States, *Government Printing Office, 1927.*)

# Contents

ix

# CONTENTS

# Introduction

WHEN I WAS GOVERNOR OF CALIFORNIA, I once had the honor of addressing the National Convention of the National Education Association. In the course of my remarks, I mentioned a number of elements I thought formed the educational birthright of every American, among them the right to be taught "the reciprocal privileges and responsibilities of American citizenship."

I had often pondered, and I continue to ponder, the question of education for good citizenship because it seems clear to me that democratic rights, privileges, freedoms—call them what you will—can survive only as long as those who exercise them do so in an informed and conscientious manner. History offers many examples of experiments in democracy that perished when the people, because of the kind of ignorance that encourages indifference, neglected the obligations of citizenship.

Yet, in our own society, how many of us take freedom for granted? How many, in moments of emotional stress, would allow some, perhaps all, of our rights to be swept away? How many, when the basic principles of our Constitution are mindlessly criticized, go along heedlessly with the critics, failing to reflect upon the extraordinary care and foresight that were responsible for its creation?

Justice Brandeis, to whom this subject was dear (he often said that "responsibility is the great developer"), wrote:

*Those who won our independence believed . . . that the greatest menace to freedom is an inert people, that public discussion is a political duty and that this should be a fundamental principle of the American Government. . . . They eschewed silence coerced by law.*

Throughout our history we have frequently overcome natural tendencies toward apathy and political inertness. And thanks to the wisdom of those who armed us with the Constitution, we have thwarted attempts to destroy freedom through coercive law. But today the attacks mount in strength and subtlety, abetted, I fear, by our failure to implant in new generations an appreciation of the Constitution and its history that can provide the best of all protections to liberty—the intelligent and independent concern of those who enjoy it.

My thoughts on so great a theme are offered to encourage others more eloquent, more persuasive, than I to recognize the practical need for concern on the part of all Americans, and to help bring to public notice simple remedies that will "secure the blessings of liberty to ourselves and our posterity."

EARL WARREN

# A Republic,
# If You Can Keep It

# I

# KEEPING
# THE REPUBLIC

D OES ANYONE doubt that a republic such as
ours, rooted in democracy, depends for its
survival on the direct, continuing and informed
participation of its citizens—all its citizens? It was
not idle rhetoric that prompted the framers of our
Constitution to begin with the words, "We, the
people." Throughout that extraordinary document
there is implicit an assumption that we, the people,
will preserve our democratic rights by acting re-
sponsibly in our enjoyment of them.

What, then, do we mean by "acting respon-
sibly"? Are we, perhaps, confronted by so many
conflicting pressures that our concern about *rights*

overshadows the *reciprocal responsibilities* without which rights can become meaningless?

It seems to me that the basic ingredient of responsible citizenship is love of country. Many, I am sure, would phrase it differently. They might call it "loyalty" or "patriotism." If we reasoned it out together, I doubt that we would find much to disagree about. I prefer "love of country" because the other terms have occasionally been adopted by extremists as labels for their own exclusive brand of "Americanism," instead of something fine and noble to which all of us can subscribe regardless of minor differences among us.

Special "labeling" follows from our modern methods of selling, whether it be cigarettes, laxatives, food or automobiles. The merits of the product itself, whatever they may be, take the form of flamboyant assertions, and become substitutes for facts and reason. Regrettably, the same methods are now applied to the selling of candidates for political office as well as to proposed solutions of public issues. Public offices were never supposed to be sold like soap or cereal. Yet campaign expenditures throughout the nation are now so enormous as to threaten the integrity of the election process itself by compromising the independence of the candidates.*

* The Citizens Research Foundation disclosed that the cost of electing the President and Vice President alone in 1968 amounted to one hundred million dollars.

Old and respected words defining political philosophy have been distorted to a degree that makes them controversial and a liability. The time-honored terms "liberal" and "conservative" have become epithets rather than philosophical designations, and have become almost synonymous with "leftist" and "reactionary." Those who oppose our engagement in foreign wars are characterized as "fair-weather patriots," "appeasers," "peaceniks," or "doves." Those who dissent, even peacefully, from the status quo in any area are advertised as "revolutionaries," "troublemakers," or "subversives." Those who would adhere to the Bill of Rights in our common cause against crime are accused of being "soft on crime" and, therefore, responsible for the lawlessness which is largely born of slums, ignorance, poverty, bad health conditions, race discrimination and lack of economic opportunity.

Extremists frame their entreaties for support in terms of slogans and epithets—or use derogatory symbols designed to overwhelm those who are not in agreement with them.

As a result, almost every issue is polarized by various catch phrases, creating divisiveness that leaves little room for adjustment to constantly changing conditions. Yet adjustment and tolerance are vital characteristics of the citizens of a democratic society. Justice Oliver Wendell Holmes said: "If there is any principle of the Constitution that more imperatively calls for attachment than any other, it is the principle of free thought—not free thought for those who agree with us but freedom for the thought that we hate."

As questionable labels are repeated again and again, the great middle group of Americans who believe in orderly progress and disdain strife become more and more wary of being catalogued in either camp. They take refuge in the anonymity of what has come to be known as the "silent majority," the majority that, as a general rule, ultimately directs the course of affairs in the nation. Most of them are home-loving people. They want to be responsible citizens. But often they despair because they don't know how they can best contribute to the fundamental interests of our nation.

In using the term "responsible citizen," I don't want to create another catch phrase to add to those I have just derided. Perhaps I should have used the word "useful" or "helpful." Either would suffice. There are 205 million of us in America and each has his own peculiar problems, his own ambitions, his own sense of proportion, and his own vision for the future. In a nation which encompasses 3,626,062 square miles, spanning a continent from the Atlantic to the Pacific, extending to the Hawaiian Islands, there is infinite room for diversity of opinion and the adjustments needed for the general good. In such a nation, there are few major issues that can be resolved in a manner satisfactory to every one of us. On the other hand, most such issues lend themselves to compromise for the ultimate betterment of the nation as a whole. We need only to apply ourselves to the task of discovering the general good rather than allow ourselves to be polarized emotionally into camps of angry protagonists and antagonists.

In suggesting the concept of "responsible citizenship," I do not mean to imply that one who does not agree entirely with what follows or does not act in accordance with it is necessarily mistaken. I am not making a moral judgment of that kind. Life in a complex society such as ours, with manifold dissimilarities of human nature as well as divergent aims and preoccupations, is such as to defy a simple catalog of attributes or a combination of activities which add up to good citizenship. It would be much easier to define irresponsible citizenship, but that is not what we are interested in. Our concern is practical and constructive: to make America a better place in which to live for ourselves and for those who are to follow us.

I began with the premise that we must have love of country. I say this not in the sense that we should be satisfied with the status quo or with the way in which our affairs are being administered at the moment. I say it in the sense that America is our home and we want it to be wholesome,

5

peaceful, dignified and satisfying for ourselves and our children, recognizing that because human nature is not perfect, government also is not perfect. Our country has shortcomings as well as virtues; it has had failures as well as successes; but it does contain all of our hopes, our ambitions, our cherished values, our treasures. And, in the words of St. Matthew 6:21, "For where your treasure is there will your heart be also."

Where there is injustice, we should correct it; where there is poverty, we should eliminate it; where there is corruption, we should stamp it out; where there is violence we should punish it; where there is neglect, we should provide care; where there is war, we should restore peace; and wherever corrections are achieved we should add them permanently to our storehouse of treasures. To me these rather obvious objectives must be above mere rhetoric; they are among the ultimate aims of the people in a democratic society.

In appraising our achievements we cannot use the measuring rod of perfection, but our judgment should be that of progress, thinking always of perfection as a goal but not necessarily as our immediate destination.

Love of country, it seems to me, is always strengthened by both a knowledge of history and a sense of history. If we have no appreciation of the past, we can have little understanding of the

6

present or vision for the future. We read of the rise and fall of nations throughout recorded time. Some achieved greatness over a long period only to lose it speedily, either because the original objectives were not attainable or because, after achieving greatness, that which was won was abandoned through neglect or arrogance. This, unfortunately, has been repeated so often that the philosopher Hegel wrote, "The only thing we learn from history is that we do not learn." And a more recent philosopher, Santayana, expanded this thought: "Those who fail to learn the lessons of history are destined to relive them."

We have come a long way as a nation and, in the perspective of history, in a very short time. Less than two hundred years ago we were the ugly duckling among the nations of the world: poor, in many places despised, reaching for a place in the sun, fighting a bloody war to achieve freedom. Since that time we have become the wealthiest and the most productive as well as the most powerful country in the world. Yet so many of our goals still elude us.

For much of what we have today, the ingenuity, the industry and the faith of our people in the future of America and our free institutions are responsible. But it must be remembered that no nation on earth at any time has ever been blessed with such an abundance of natural resources. So,

for us to envision the future of our nation and what
our responsibilities are in shaping it, we must know
where we came from; how we arrived where we are
today; what we see as our ultimate destination and
by what means we can best reach it.

The problems confronting us are almost without number and are becoming more complex and
aggravated by the growth of our intricate economic
system, the population explosion and the incredi-
ble facility of communication between every part
of the globe. But, in pondering their solutions, one
of the aphorisms of Justice Holmes becomes perti-
nent: "A page of history is worth a volume of
logic."

# II

# CREATING A NATION

SEPTEMBER 17, 1787, is an important day in the life of our nation—perhaps as important as any other in our history. It was on that day that the Constitutional Convention adjourned after the signing of the draft of the proposed Constitution under which we have lived for almost two centuries.

The delegates had labored for one hundred sixteen days throughout the long, hot and humid Philadelphia summer. Although the exact number is somewhat in doubt, it has been generally reported that seventy-four delegates were elected or appointed from twelve colonies. (Rhode Island refused to send any delegates.) But only fifty-five of the seventy-four appeared at Independence Hall

9

where the Declaration of Independence had been signed eleven years before; and many of these left sometime during the summer either because of health or in disagreement with the proceedings or in the belief that the objective could not be achieved.

The differences of opinion were marked and necessitated many compromises before the various provisions could be acceded to by a majority of the delegates. It is difficult to say what the outcome would have been were it not for the fervent plea written by the elder statesman Benjamin Franklin, immediately prior to the signing. In order to achieve unanimity and to present a united front to the nation, he urged that all of the delegates, in a spirit of compromise, attach their signatures to the proposed Constitution. James Wilson, a delegate from Pennsylvania, read Franklin's statement aloud, addressing George Washington, the President of the Convention:

*I confess that there are several parts of the Constitution which I do not at present approve; but I am not sure I shall never approve them. For, having lived long, I have experienced many instances of being obliged, by better information, or fuller consideration, to change opinions even on important subjects, which I once thought right, but found to be otherwise. It is, therefore, that the older I grow, the more apt I am to doubt my own judgment, and to pay more respect to the judgment of others. . . . Thus, I consent, Sir, to this Constitution because I expect no better, and because I am not sure that it is not the best. . . . On the whole, Sir, I cannot help expressing a wish that every member of the Convention who may still have objections to it, would, with me, on this occasion doubt a little of his own infallibility;—and to make manifest our unanimity, put his name to this instrument.*

To our lasting benefit, thirty-nine delegates, representing twelve states, signed and adjourned to have their handiwork presented to the nation for its approval.

It was at this moment that a woman approached Benjamin Franklin with her anxious question: "Well, Doctor, what have we got, a republic or a monarchy?"

And he replied, "A republic, if you can keep it."

The incident was recorded by Dr. James McHenry, who gave the name of the lady as a "Mrs. Powel of Phila.," but unfortunately, there is no way for us to know just how much of Franklin's cryptic answer she understood. At that time there was not another republic in existence nor had there been for many centuries, and the cryptic phrase, "If you can keep it," probably had very little significance for her. But the importance of this historic exchange is that Franklin was saying that the new Constitution gave the ultimate responsibility for its success to the people.

Franklin was a wise man; indeed, he was often called "the wisest American." He had lived a long life and had served the colonies and the new nation for decades in many capacities. He was a philosopher, diplomat and scientist, and had moved in the highest circles both at home and abroad. He had seen life in Paris under the autocratic reign of Louis XVI and Marie Antoinette which a few years later culminated in the French Revolution. He had represented our new nation in London during the reign of George III, whose arbitrary colonial policies had driven the American colonies to revolt.

Franklin was well aware that there was little democracy in the world at that time. But there had been democracies and republics, even before the Christian Era. They had all disappeared, and he knew why. He knew that whenever a democratic government had failed, it was because the people had abdicated their responsibility. And he also knew that democracy had invariably been supplanted by an authoritarian regime which denied the people all right to govern themselves.

The survival of the republic which the proposed Constitution would establish depended, Franklin was certain, upon the willingness of the people as citizens to support it. A republic is not an easy form of government to live under, and when the responsibility of citizenship is evaded, democracy decays and authoritarianism takes over. It is this basic and vital concept of responsibility to which his words, "if you can keep it," referred.

To appreciate the full import of those words, however, it is necessary to know what preceded the Constitutional Convention, why it was held, and the problems to which the delegates addressed themselves.

The first English colony at Jamestown, Virginia, was founded in 1607. The original colonists had come to this new continent for a variety of reasons—religious, political or economic—but all were looking for a new life in freedom.* It was not only a small beginning; it was a humble beginning,

---

* In 1957, as a part of the 350th anniversary celebration of the founding of Virginia, replicas of the three little ships (which had landed as variously reported either 104 or 144 colonists) anchored in the Potomac River at Washington, D.C., before going on to the peninsula in the James River, the site of the first English colony. Looking at these tiny craft, it is difficult to believe that they carried all of the settlers to America's first colony on the North American continent.

13

because most of the early colonists were poor as were those who later settled there.

Life was hard and in the first year all but thirty-eight of the colonists died before supplies and more settlers arrived in 1608. As late as 1641, when the population had grown to above 7,500, three fourths of those who had come to Jamestown were indentured servants or apprentices. Only courage and fortitude kept them alive.

In 1609, the London Company to which the colony had been chartered as a commercial venture had its charter extended 400 miles along the Atlantic Coast and west from "Sea to Sea." Land was then sold to the settlers, as a result of which not only the plantation economy developed but also a western migration. And, with the permission of the Company, the colonists took their first step in local government in 1619 through the establishment of a House of Burgesses. In 1624, Virginia became a Royal Colony, the first in English history.

The next colony to be established in the New World was Plymouth, also under charter from the London Company. In the summer of 1620, the Pilgrims sailed for Virginia from Plymouth, England, in the *Mayflower*. In November, they sighted the coast of Cape Cod instead of Virginia. They explored the coastline for five weeks and, though they realized that they were not in the area granted them by charter, finally landed. Before stepping ashore they wrote and signed a significant agreement known as the Mayflower Compact. This was the first self-initiated act of government on the new continent. It was a simple document, written by plain people, but it contained lasting wisdom. The two hundred-odd words of the Mayflower Compact remained the solid basis for the government of the colony for some seventy years until it became united with the Massachusetts Bay colony in 1691:

IN THE NAME OF GOD, AMEN. *We, whose names are underwritten, the Loyal Subjects of our dread Sovereign Lord King James, by the Grace of God, of* Great Britain, France, *and* Ireland, *King,* Defender of the Faith, *&c. Having undertaken for the Glory of God, and Advancement of the Christian Faith, and the Honour of our King and Country, a Voyage to plant the first Colony in the northern Parts of Virginia; Do by these Presents, solemnly and mutually in the Presence of God and one another, covenant and combine ourselves together into a civil Body Politick, for our better Ordering and Preservation, and Furtherance of the Ends aforesaid: And by Virtue hereof do enact, constitute and frame, such just and equal Laws, Ordinances, Acts, Constitutions, and Offices, from time to time, as shall be thought most meet and convenient for the general Good of the Colony;*

15

*unto which we promise all due Submission and Obedience. IN WITNESS whereof we have hereunto subscribed our names at* Cape-Cod *the eleventh of* November, *in the Reign of our Sovereign Lord King James, of* England, France *and* Ireland, *the eighteenth, and of Scotland, the fifty-fourth, anno domini, 1620.*

The Pilgrims suffered much the same as the settlers at Jamestown. In the first year, about half of them died. The growth of the colony was slow, and to improve life many of them explored the unknown country to the north and west in search of better farmland.

The stories of Virginia and Plymouth emphasize the fact that from the day the first settlers arrived on this new and unknown continent they were thinking of self-government and of how to achieve it, even though at the time they were desperately struggling for life itself.

Successively, England established other colonies until at the time of the American Revolution there were thirteen. Those in the north, grouped in an area called New England, included New Hampshire, Massachusetts, Rhode Island and Connecticut; the middle colonies consisted of New York, New Jersey, Pennsylvania, Delaware and Maryland; and Georgia, North Carolina, South Carolina and Virginia made up the southern colonies. Most of the commercial and manufacturing centers were concentrated in the middle colonies, while the south was almost entirely agricultural. At the time of the Revolution, 95 per cent of all Americans were farmers.

As the colonists migrated westward, they became less attached to the mother country and thought more in terms of controlling their own affairs. Many differences of opinion developed between the colonies and the British Government. The colonists were pressing more and more to govern themselves. And the Royal Governors and their henchmen were, in many instances, purely political appointees without any knowledge or understanding of the country they were coming to or of the people whom they were to govern. Their often arbitrary actions forced the colonists to grow farther and farther apart from the homeland, not necessarily because they wanted to be free from England, but because they resented being deprived of the rights that Englishmen at home enjoyed.

Disagreements multiplied through the years, but until 1765 they did not become abrasive, and the colonists gave little thought to separation from the homeland. But when the Parliament passed the Sugar Act in 1764 and the Stamp Act in 1765 (which imposed a tax on all legal documents and newspapers), there was violent reaction.

17

The phrase "No Taxation without Representation" became a rallying cry and, in the end, Parliament repealed the Stamp Act.

This temporarily allayed the fears of the colonists until, in 1767, the Parliament enacted more tax measures against them and, in an effort to punish the Massachusetts Colony for the Boston Tea Party, passed the so-called Intolerable Acts or Coercive Acts in 1774. There were five acts: one closed the Port of Boston until such time as the East India Company should be paid for the tea destroyed; others changed the provisions of the Massachusetts Charter to authorize the quartering of Royal troops without provincial consent, and also to give Royal officials in conflict with colonial authorities the right to trial in England.* In particular, the Quebec Act, which limited the right of Massachusetts to expand into the northwest, aroused all of the colonies since it raised the threat of such restriction to any colony. Not only could it deprive them of the right to administer their own local laws; it could become a precedent for the violation of the "Sea to Sea" grants of many colonial charters.

These Acts embittered the colonists to the extent that they realized the necessity of having a continental association which could speak for all of the

---

* The quartering of troops led to the protection against such intrusion in the Third Amendment in our Bill of Rights.

colonies in their relation with the British Government. The result was the First Continental Congress, convened in Philadelphia on September 5, 1774. Delegates attended from all the colonies except Georgia. Although the temper of the Congress was at fever pitch, comparatively few people were thinking of independence from the mother country. The primary objective was the redress of wrongs.

Nevertheless, there were provocative actions taken. The Continental Association was created which forbade the use of British goods and proposed prohibition of colonial exports. Petitions of grievances were sent to the King, and the Congress was adjourned until May 10, 1775, in the event that the grievances should not be adjusted.

It met again on that date, only three weeks after the Battles of Lexington and Concord where the shots fired were "heard round the world." Although there was more sentiment in favor of independence at this gathering, the Congress was still not yet ready for such drastic action. It did, however, create a Continental Army to oppose the British, and, on June 15, 1775, George Washington was appointed Commander-in-Chief. Although there was not a formal declaration—and there never would be—the War of the American Revolution was now a very real one.

After a year of skirmishes in various colonies,

the Congress again met in Philadelphia and, on July 4, 1776, in the Declaration of Independence, proclaimed to the world the colonies' separation from England and the establishment of the United States of America. The thirteen colonies thus became the United States and, under the most adverse circumstances, fought the War of the Revolution to a successful conclusion on October 19, 1781, when Lord Cornwallis surrendered to George Washington at Yorktown.

# III

# THE CONSTITUTION
# AND BILL OF RIGHTS

D URING THE YEARS of the War of the Revolution, the affairs of the colonists were administered by the Continental Congress. There was no
other national agency, and its powers over the
colonies were extremely limited. It served another
important purpose, however. It established in the
minds of all that a loose confederacy could not
guide the nation either at home or in its relations
with the rest of the world. The powers of the
Congress were somewhat expanded by the Articles
of Confederation in 1781, but it was still unable
to enforce its actions on the individual states even
though it was stated that the Union should be

perpetual and to that end the Articles "shall be inviolably observed."

As soon as the war ended, the disparate interests of the states, stemming largely from differences in their economies, came to the forefront. Long-standing jealousies surfaced; acquisitiveness, particularly relating to conflicting claims to Western lands, often became the determining factor in the relationship between the states. Since the government had no power to compel the states to observe national treaty obligations, there was little respect accorded to it by foreign nations. Other nations looked with envious eyes at several of the states and were hopeful that the new confederation would collapse and its parts become available for their aggrandizement.

National debts were neither paid nor funded, and our money deteriorated. It became evident to thoughtful men—and there were many such in the states—that a more efficient government had to be established to prevent dissolution. These men were students of the eighteenth-century liberal thought in Europe: that of Locke and Hobbes in England, and of Montesquieu, Rousseau and Voltaire in France. They were also, of course, aware that, since the Declaration of Independence, there was feverish activity throughout the colonies to write constitutions which would enable each of them to govern their affairs independently. It was not uncommon for people, in speaking of their state, to use the expression "my country."

As early as 1772, in Massachusetts, committees of correspondence had been established to try to achieve unity of action among the colonies. After the war, and the proven ineffectiveness of the Articles of Confederation, men like Washington, Jefferson, Madison, Franklin and Hamilton used their great influence to hold a national convention. Such a convention was called by Virginia in 1786, largely at the instigation of commercial interests, but representatives of only a few of the colonies appeared and it was adjourned without action. In the following year, as conditions worsened, Congress was induced to call a convention to meet in Philadelphia on May 14, 1787, "for the sole and express purpose of revising the Articles of Confederation."

While most of the fifty-five delegates who attended were favorable to the general purpose of the convention, they held widely differing views as to how the government should be constructed. In Virginia, the elected delegates were in such conflict that while James Madison attended every session, Patrick Henry bitterly refused to come to the convention at all. Alexander Hamilton was the only delegate from New York who remained to sign the draft. Unfortunately, two stalwart supporters of the convention could not be present for its deliberations—Thomas Jefferson was in Paris arranging for commercial treaties, and John Adams was in London. Nevertheless, they were diligent in their correspondence, which was helpful to the cause.

The final draft of the Constitution did not represent the plan of any delegate or group of delegates. Rather, it was a series of adjustments and compromises that reorganized the strongly held principles of these leaders of the fledgling nation.

Yet there was even difficulty in forming a consensus regarding the implementation of these principles. Because of their colonial experience, the delegates had come not only to distrust power but to hate it, and they were determined to diffuse it as much as possible and still leave a viable government for the nation. They feared a central government, and were intent upon a division of powers between it and the various states. They determined that it should be essentially a government of the people, and that all power not delegated to the government should be retained by them.

They also were enamored of the doctrine of the separation of powers, and used it to control the federal government by dividing its powers among its three branches—the legislative, the executive and the judicial—with what they considered appropriate checks and balances to insure against abuse by any one of them.

When the document was completed perhaps

24

the main point of agreement among the delegates was that the power to govern should be diffused through a federal system which left in the people the ultimate responsibility of determining their own affairs through duly elected representatives. It was essentially an American document created out of the experience and the culture of the various states and exhibiting an awareness of the opportunities for expansion by a new nation on an unexplored continent. In effect, it made the people the ultimate guardian of its future.

I use the word "people" because, as I pointed out before, the Preamble to the Constitution says:

*We, the People of the United States, in Order to form a more perfect Union, establish Justice, insure domestic Tranquility, provide for the common defense, promote the general Welfare, and secure the Blessings of Liberty to ourselves and our Posterity, do ordain and establish this Constitution for the United States of America.*

It noticeably does not say "We the citizens of the United States"; nor does it define a citizen of the United States. It mentions that the elective officers of the United States shall be citizens of the United States, but nowhere does it define the meaning of citizenship. So far as can be ascertained, the words "citizen" and "people" were used interchangeably, because there was no commonly accepted definition of either.

At the time of our Revolution, each colony had different qualifications for citizenship, many of which depended upon landed property and religious qualifications. There were no national standards, and the specter which haunted the Constitutional Convention in this regard was slavery. Slavery was debated tangentially in relation to the manner in which slaves should be counted for the purpose of taxation and representation in the Congress. It was finally decided that each slave should be counted as three-fifths of a person. The question of slavery was also implicit in a provision that Congress shall not prohibit the "migration or importation of such persons as any of the states now existing shall think proper to admit . . . prior to the year 1808, but a tax or duty may be imposed on such importation not exceeding $10.00 for each person." In plain words Congress, although empowered generally to "regulate commerce" with foreign nations, was prohibited from interfering with the slave traffic for twenty years, though it did require the return of fugitive slaves who fled to another state.

The treatment of the slavery question was, of course, inconsistent with the ringing words of the Declaration of Independence that "all men are created equal, that they are endowed by their

Creator with certain unalienable rights, that among these are life, liberty and the pursuit of happiness." But the delegates realized that slavery was almost a forbidden subject and that any attempt to resolve the controversial situation would bring about the dissolution of the Convention. As a result, the Constitution was written in the most general of terms, with the expectation and belief that it represented basic principles which could be implemented into the indefinite future.

When the Constitution was sent to the Congress and thereafter printed in the press, the nation was startled. Even those who were strongly in favor of a more effective national government had little reason to expect that such a comprehensive document would emerge from the Convention's deliberations, since the Congress had merely authorized the Convention to "revise the Articles of Confederation." Congress itself was taken aback and presented it to the states without giving the document its forthright approval. Ratification by nine states was necessary before it could become effective, and the Convention required that such ratification be accomplished by special Ratifying conventions elected by the people in each state, bypassing the regularly elected state legislatures.

The first state to consider it, little Delaware, promptly adopted it unanimously, as did New Jersey and Georgia. But in most of the other states the fights for ratification were vigorous and covered the entire spectrum of emotion. It was praised greatly by many and vilified by others.

Patrick Henry, the great Virginia Revolutionary orator, opposed it with all his might:

*Whither is the spirit of America gone? Whither is the genius of America fled? . . . We drew the spirit of liberty from our British ancestors. But now, Sir, the American spirit, assisted by the ropes and chains of consolidation, is about to convert this country into a powerful and mighty empire. . . . There will be no checks, no real balances, in this government. What can avail your specious, imaginary balances, your rope-dancing, chain-rattling, ridiculous ideal checks and contrivances?*

Thomas Jefferson gave his strong approval in a letter to Madison from Paris in 1888:

*It is a good canvas on which some strokes only want retouching.*

And in explication later, he wrote to David Humphreys:

*The operations which have taken place in America lately fill me with pleasure . . . The ex-*

28

*ample of changing a Constitution by assembling the wise men of the State instead of assembling armies will be worth as much to the world as former examples we have given them. The Constitution . . . is unquestionably the wisest ever presented to men . . .*

In Massachusetts, the final vote for adoption was 187 to 168; in New Hampshire it was 57 to 46; in New York 30 to 27; in Virginia 89 to 79; and in Pennsylvania 46 to 23. Within nine months it was ratified by all the states except Rhode Island and North Carolina (which later did so), and on September 13, 1788, the Congress, by resolution, recognized it.

The story of the Constitutional Convention and the ratification of the Constitution is fascinating. Strangely enough, it has not been brought to the attention of the American public as forcefully or as dramatically as other aspects of American history. Yet, to understand what is going on today it is of extreme importance that every American should have an appreciation of the problems which brought the Convention into being; the men who composed it; the driving forces behind each of them; the compromises they were obliged to make in order to achieve a consensus; and their patience and indefatigability in achieving the desired end.*

* The entire story is delightfully told in *Miracle at Philadelphia* by

Perhaps the most pragmatic view of the Constitution was that of Justice Oliver Wendell Holmes a century or so later, in his statement that "the Constitution was an experiment as all life is an experiment." But undoubtedly the true witness of its greatness is that within twenty-five years after its adoption many other countries used it as a guide in drafting their own Constitutions.

One might suppose that constitution-making was at an end when the states adopted the provisions created by the Convention. But some of the gravest problems which would confront the new nation were deliberately left to another day. Jefferson, one of the strongest advocates of the Constitution, also recognized the great importance of a bill of rights:

*I wish with all my soul that the nine first conventions may accept the new Constitution, because this will secure to us the good it contains which I think great and important. But I equally wish that the four latest conventions, whichever they may be, may refuse to accede to it till a declaration of rights be annexed. This would probably command the offer of such a declaration, and thus give to the whole fabric, perhaps as much perfection as any one of that kind ever had.*

Catherine Drinker Bowen. I believe it would benefit every American to read it.

There were others, like Hamilton, who believed that because certain rights were guaranteed under the English system the preservation of those rights would be implicit in any American constitution. Undoubtedly, there were still others who either did not believe at all in such a bill of rights or were apprehensive about subjecting them to debate at such a critical time.

Nevertheless, the need could not be ignored. The Massachusetts Convention ratified the Constitution only after an agreement was reached to propose the immediate inclusion of a bill of rights. It did not make its ratification dependent upon it, but it left no doubt as to its insistence that such an addition should be made. Virginia followed the same course, and suggested adapting the bill of rights from its own state constitution, an idea that had the support of both Jefferson and Madison.

In New York the fight for the Constitution was almost lost over the issue: Hamilton insisted to the end that "the Constitution is itself in every rational sense, and to every useful purpose, a Bill of Rights," and that a specific bill of rights was not necessary.

But the clamor for such a bill could not be denied. In the First Congress in 1789 James Madison immediately introduced constitutional amendments to clarify certain individual and state rights not named in the Constitution. In the preamble to the resolution offering the proposed amendments to the states, Congress said:

*The Conventions of a number of the states having, at the time of their adopting the Constitution, expressed a desire, in order to prevent misconstruction or abuse of its powers, that further declaratory and restrictive clauses should be added, and as extending the ground of public confidence in the government will best insure the beneficient ends of its institution, be it resolved. . . .*

Ten of Madison's twelve amendments were ratified by the states and became effective on December 25, 1791. They were thereafter known as the Bill of Rights, and their provisions have become the sacred rights of the American people without which we would have had a form of free government but not the substance of our freedom.*

For almost two hundred years these amendments have been interpreted by our courts in thousands of cases in a manner to protect the rights guaranteed therein to the people. In the aggregate, these cases represent the principal part of our constitutional law and are perhaps the best illustration of the far-reaching effect of the broad but controlling language used in the Constitution.

---

* See Chapters X and XII for a detailed discussion of the provisions of the Bill of Rights.

# IV

# LONG STRUGGLE FOR CITIZENSHIP

E VEN WITH the adoption of the Bill of Rights, there were still nebulous and undefined areas in the Constitution. The principal one, of course, was the determination of who constituted the citizens of the United States and what made them such citizens. The ominous existence of slavery complicated the problem of citizenship, in such a manner as to defy solution.

Although the words "citizen" and "citizenship" have been used throughout much of history, they have meant different things at different times and in different countries. In the ancient Athenian city-states, the basis of citizenship was property. In the Roman Empire all free men were citizens. During the Dark Ages and feudal times, citizenship became nonexistent until the time when cities were granted some immunities from feudal dues and were permitted the basic rudiments of local government. Citizenship really began to take on its modern connotations after the American and French revolutions.

Prior to our Revolution, citizenship was a matter for the British government and the individual states. An Englishman who migrated to a colony was, of course, a citizen of that colony, and if he moved to another he automatically became a citizen of that colony. But for those who were not British citizens each colony had its own naturalization procedure to which immigrants had to conform, and migration from one colony to another did not necessarily carry citizenship from the former to the latter. Immediately before the Declaration of Independence, on June 6, 1776, the Continental Congress resolved that "All persons abiding within any of the united colonies and deriving protection from the laws of the same owe allegiance to the said laws and are members of such colony."

After the Declaration of Independence, individual states began to enact laws defining citizenship and establishing naturalization proceedings. These procedures were not uniform and varied greatly in their requirements. Some stipulated residence for a term of years; Virginia, on the other hand, asked only that a foreigner reside in the state and take an oath of fidelity in order to acquire every right of a native citizen. Difficulties between the states arose on this issue, but the Continental Congress could do little about it. Each state, acting as an independent republic, issued its own passports signed by its own officials.

While the Constitution mentioned "citizen of the United States" without uniformly defining what that meant, it did state that before a person could be President or a Senator or a member of the House of Representatives he must have been a citizen of the United States for a definite period of time. In Section 2 of Article IV, it put the general burden of determining national citizenship on the states by providing that "the citizens of each state shall be entitled to all privileges and immunities of citizens in the several states." The Constitution left the federal government one option, however, in the provision that Congress shall have the power "to establish a uniform Rule of Naturalization" (subject to one unavoidable qualification—that traffic in slaves would not be prohibited for twenty years).

Acting under that power, Congress immediately provided for the naturalization of any *free white persons* who had resided for two years "within the limits and under the jurisdiction of the

United States," and authorized the proceedings to be conducted in "any common law court of record in any one of the states."

But there was a large population of men and women who could not become citizens under any existing law, whether federal or state. They were the slaves, and the bitter debate over their condition created one crisis after another, involving both the rights of individuals and, in particular, the admission of new states to the Union. Some states had already elected to abolish slavery; others were violently opposed to freeing the slaves. The so-called Missouri Compromise in 1820 was designed to mollify both the slave owner and the abolitionist by admitting Maine to the Union as a free state and Missouri as a slave state, but prohibiting slavery in the remainder of the Missouri Territory north of the extended southern boundary of the new State of Missouri.

The debate erupted again over the admission of California to statehood in 1850, and reached the crisis stage in 1854 when the Kansas and Nebraska territories were being organized. Both of the proposed states were in the area in which slavery had been prohibited by the Missouri Compromise. Many of the Kansas people had come from slave states, particularly Missouri, and were in favor of a slave economy. The sentiment in the territory, however, was sharply divided. In Nebraska, there was little doubt that the people there would want to establish a free state. The tension grew, and Congress had to repeal the Missouri Compromise which would have prohibited slavery in Kansas, and provided that "all questions pertaining to slavery in the territories and in the new states to be therefrom, are to be left to the people residing therein, through their appropriate representatives."

When President Pierce signed the bill, the militant, antislavery Senator from Massachusetts, Charles Sumner, made a prophetic appraisal: "It is at once the worst and best Bill on which Congress ever acted—the worst inasmuch as it is a present victory for slavery, and the best for it annuls all past compromises with slavery and makes all future compromises impossible. Thus it puts freedom and slavery face to face, and bids them grapple. Who can doubt the result?"

One result was that slavery was now possible in still more territory to the west. Instead of allaying the controversy, the new law accelerated it greatly, and brought about violent disorder in Kansas where two state governments, "both illegalized by fraud and violence," were established.

Before either Kansas or Nebraska was actually admitted, however, the issue of slavery became personified in the *Dred Scott* case, and convulsed an already anguished nation.

Scott was a Negro, born in slavery in the slave

state of Virginia and later taken into the slave state of Missouri. In 1834, he went with his master, an Army medical officer, to Illinois, a free state, and from there to what later became the State of Minnesota, a free territory under the provisions of the Missouri Compromise. Here he married and had a daughter before the family was taken back to Missouri by the master in 1838.

After the death of his master, Scott filed suit in the State of Missouri against the widow claiming freedom for himself and his family—his wife and two children—on the ground that his residence in the free state of Illinois and the free territory relieved him of his bondage. He prevailed at first but lost his case in the Supreme Court of Missouri. He sued again for the same relief in the United States Circuit Court for the District of Missouri, where the decision also went against him. He then appealed to the Supreme Court of the United States.

Chief Justice Taney, speaking for the Court, held that a free Negro of the African race whose ancestors were brought to this country and sold as slaves is not a "citizen" within the meaning of the Constitution of the United States. He held further that "it has been settled by the decisions of the highest court in Missouri, that, by the laws of that State, a slave does not become entitled to his freedom, where the owner takes him to reside in a State where slavery is not permitted, and afterwards brings him back to Missouri." He concluded that the Congress had no power to prevent slavery in the territories and, accordingly, held the Missouri Compromise to have been unconstitutional.

In effect, the Court opened up to slavery the territory all the way to the Pacific Coast without any power in the Congress to prevent it. This decision caused a rapid deterioration in the relationship between the Northern and Southern states, and is generally considered one of the causes of the Civil War. It is a case that Chief Justice Charles Evans Hughes years later listed as one of the "self-inflicted wounds" of the Supreme Court.

An effort was made by Southerners to re-establish the slave trade and also to establish "Black Codes" recognizing slavery in all its forms throughout the nation. When these efforts were defeated, there developed a decided drift toward secession. On December 20, 1860, a little more than a month after the election of Abraham Lincoln, the South Carolina Legislature unanimously declared that "The Union now subsisting between South Carolina and the other states under the name of 'the United States of America' is hereby dissolved." Similar sentiment was strong throughout the cotton states, and before Lincoln was inaugurated on March 4, 1861, the entire South had so acted. Many military establishments were taken over, as well as customs houses and other United States facilities. The first shots were fired at Fort Sumter, South Carolina, on April 12, 1861, where Lincoln had decided to make the initial show of resistance.

Then followed the most traumatic experience the nation has ever suffered—four years of fratricidal warfare resulting in the death of one out of every ten young men of military age. While it was essentially a war of conflicting ways of life, it did not command universal support for either side in any part of the country.* Hundreds of thousands of families, particularly in the border and western states and territories, were torn apart and pitted against each other in mortal combat.

This is not the place to retell the oft-repeated story of that war, but we cannot be reminded too

---

* The crossing of lines is graphically stated as follows in *The Growth of the American Republic* by Morison and Commager, Vol. 1, p. 621:

*Throughout the Civil War, lines were never strictly drawn between the states that seceded and those that did not. The United States Army and Navy contained loyal men from every seceded state, Americans who knew that the break-up of the Union would be the worst blow to the cause of self-government and republicanism since the day that Bonaparte assumed the purple. Admiral Farragut was born in Tennessee; General George Thomas was born in Virginia, and so too the Commander in Chief of the Union Forces, General Winfield Scott, Samuel P. Lee commanded the Union naval forces on the James River while his uncle, General Robert E. Lee, was resisting Grant in the Wilderness. Two sons of Commodore Porter, USN, fought under Stonewall Jackson; Senator Crittenden of the attempted compromise had two sons, Major General T. L. Crittenden, USA, and Major General G. B. Crittenden, CSA. Three brothers of Mrs. Lincoln died for the South, and the President's kinsmen on his mother's side were Southern sympathizers, whilst near kinsmen of Mrs. Davis were in the Union Army.*

often of its ferocity and deadly effect. Of the Union forces, 364,000 gave up their lives in combat or from other war-related causes, and 281,000 were wounded. On the Confederate side, 138,000 died. There are no authoritative statistics concerning the number wounded in the Confederate Army, but undoubtedly the total number of casualties on both sides reached 1,000,000. And the real tragedy is that all of these casualties were suffered by Americans fighting for what they believed was necessary to preserve their conception of the free way of life.

Throughout the long struggle, the man most sickened by the carnage but determined that the Union should not be broken up, was the loneliest man in the nation: the President of the United States, Abraham Lincoln. He accepted temporary victories and defeats alike with sadness and compassion for all. His profound beliefs and uncompromising principles were stated in his memorable address dedicating the military cemetery on the site of the Battle of Gettysburg, Pennsylvania—perhaps the greatest battle and the turning point of the war, where each side had in the neighborhood of 20,000 casualties. The address was really a two-minute postscript to the speech lasting two hours given by the famous orator, Senator Edward Everett of Massachusetts. Yet it is one of the classics of American literature and is known in all parts of the world. Of the address, Senator Everett wrote to Lincoln, "I should be glad if I could flatter myself that I came as close to the central case in two hours as you did in two minutes." For Americans, repetition of Lincoln's Gettysburg Address is never out of order—

*Four score and seven years ago our fathers brought forth on this continent, a new nation, conceived in Liberty, and dedicated to the proposition that all men are created equal.*

*Now we are engaged in a great civil war, testing whether that nation or any nation so conceived and so dedicated, can long endure. We are met on a great battle-field of that war. We have come to dedicate a portion of that field, as a final resting place for those who here gave their lives that that nation might live. It is altogether fitting and proper that we should do this.*

*But, in a larger sense, we cannot dedicate— we cannot consecrate—we cannot hallow this ground. The brave men, living and dead, who struggled here, have consecrated it, far above our poor power to add or detract. The world will little note, nor long remember what we say here, but it can never forget what they did here. It is for us the living, rather, to be dedicated here to the unfinished work which they who fought here have thus far so nobly advanced. It is rather for us to be here dedicated to the great task remaining before us—that from these honored dead we take increased devotion to that cause for which they gave the last full measure of devotion—that we here highly resolve that these dead shall not have died in vain—and that this nation, under God, shall have a new birth of freedom—and that government of the people, by the people, for the people, shall not perish from the earth.*

The war raged on until April 9, 1865, when the great Confederate General, Robert E. Lee, his forces exhausted and entrapped, surrendered at Appomatox Courthouse to General Ulysses S. Grant.

But tragedy still stalked the nation. Five days after Lee's surrender, Abraham Lincoln was assassinated, and the nation was bereft of its compassionate leader who only six weeks before his death closed his second inaugural address with this pledge:

*With malice toward none, with charity for all, with firmness in the right as God gives us to see the right, let us strive on to finish the work we are in, to bind up the nation's wounds, to care for him who shall have fought the battle and for his widow and his orphan, to do all which may achieve and cherish a just and lasting peace among ourselves and with all nations.*

No longer could he "bind up the nation's wounds." In the words of Secretary of War Stanton, "Now he belongs to the ages."

The republic Benjamin Franklin described as he left the Constitutional Convention had been kept—but at what a price.

The Reconstruction period which followed was another turbulent and divisive era, and a leader such as the simple and compassionate Lincoln was badly needed to keep the ship of state on an even keel between a peculiarly American Scylla and Charybdis—the rock occupied by the six-headed monster of slavery in the South and the whirlpool of revenge on the part of extremists in the North.

Out of the conflict, however, came the right of citizenship for all Americans in the form of the Thirteenth, Fourteenth and Fifteenth Amendments to the Constitution. Before Lincoln's death, the Congress had submitted to the states the Thirteenth Amendment, which abolished slavery throughout the nation forever. It was declared ratified December 18, 1865. Section I reads:

*Neither slavery nor involuntary servitude, except as a punishment for crime whereof the party shall have been duly convicted, shall exist within the United States, or any place subject to their jurisdiction.*

44

Thus, the institution of slavery was buried, as it had already been by most of the nations of the world.

The next year Congress proposed the Fourteenth Amendment, which, among other things, finally defined "citizens of the United States." It was declared ratified and came into force on July 28, 1868. Section I of that amendment provides:

*All persons born or naturalized in the United States, and subject to the jurisdiction thereof, are citizens of the United States and of the State wherein they reside. No State shall make or enforce any law which shall abridge the privileges or immunities of citizens of the United States; nor shall any State deprive any person of life, liberty, or property, without due process of law; nor deny to any person within its jurisdiction the equal protection of the laws.*

Still concerned about the right of the people to participate in their government, and to be rid of the last vestiges of slavery, the Congress submitted yet another amendment to the Constitution, the Fifteenth. On March 30, 1870, having been ratified by the requisite number of states, the amendment was declared to be in force. Section I reads:

*The right of citizens of the United States to vote shall not be denied or abridged by the United States or by any State on account of race, color, or previous condition of servitude.*

Thus, with these three amendments, the omissions of the original Constitution regarding citizenship were supplied, and the distortions of the *Dred Scott* case and the Kansas-Nebraska Act were obliterated. From that day, there has been but one kind of citizenship—citizenship of the United States—regardless of the state of residence, and with the reinforcement that "No State shall make or enforce any act which shall abridge the privileges or immunities of citizens of the United States. . . ."

But this was not the end to the problem of citizenship although it should have been. Throughout the years numerous efforts have been made in some quarters to dilute this citizenship by denying a multitude of rights to minority groups, because of race, color or national origin. Among other things they were denied the right to travel except under substandard and humiliating conditions such as "Jim Crow" buses and trains; the right to live where they desire; the right of a good education because of segregated and grossly inadequate schools; the right to use public accommodations such as hotels, restaurants, thea-

46

ters, and the stations of railroads, buses and airlines; and the right to use public parks or beaches paid for from the taxes of all the people. Their right to vote was jeopardized by discriminatory laws and procedures preventing minority voter registration. They were even denied the right to sit quietly in a courtroom unless relegated to a segregated section denoting inferiority, or to be addressed while there by court and counsel as Miss, Mrs. or Mr. as are white witnesses and parties to litigation. They have not been allowed to have people of their own race considered for jury service in cases wherein they are parties and have been compelled to testify against themselves through coerced confessions. These rights—all of them—are basic and "unalienable" to American citizenship, and have repeatedly been so announced by the Supreme Court of the United States.

But the road to such decisions has been a tortuous one. Even in criminal cases which involve life imprisonment people have been denied, because of their poverty, the right to be represented by counsel.* Without these rights there is no real

---

* One is justified in wondering why, since the Supreme Court has established these principles under the Constitution, they are not observed more uniformly. The answer rests in part upon the nature of the judicial process. The Supreme Court, like other courts, is limited to deciding actual "cases and controversies." A change in circumstances or a new circumventing statute offers an opportunity to relitigate the issue in the light of these changes; but often the poor litigants either succumb to the oppression or are forced to spend years trying to vindicate themselves. This, taken with the fact that the ingenuity of those who are

freedom, and if any group can be deprived of them the same situation can befall other groups at other times and under other conditions. The only protection of every citizen from such deprivation of rights is a strict adherence to the Bill of Rights by everyone for everyone. This should be self-evident, but the danger of erosion of rights stems largely from the fact that so many citizens of the majority, who have never been deprived of any of these rights, find it difficult to understand what the deprivation of them means in the lives of others.

---

determined not to accord equal rights to all is limited only by their imaginations, results in a maze of time-consuming and frustrating litigation to achieve those rights.

# V

# PROBLEMS OF A
# MULTIRACIAL SOCIETY

THE BUILDING of our country is unmatched in world history. It was brought about in the main by poor people who pioneered, pressing ever westward from the Atlantic shore. In the early days, they were confronted with every kind of danger and natural barrier, but these they overcame. They cleared land for the plow, built cities and industries, developed means of communication, moving always onward until they reached the Pacific Ocean. It was confidence in their ability to conquer the unknown that impelled them 3,000 miles to the West. It was always faith and not fear that drove them. So rugged were their treks that in the Far West there was a saying: "The timid never started, and the weak died on the way."

As our country expanded beyond the Appalachian Mountains toward the West, we needed people to develop our land and to man our industry. Throughout the Industrial Revolution, we appealed to people all over the world to come here and build with us a land of freedom. Since 1820, when the first immigration figures were recorded, forty-five million people from almost every country have responded to the call. In the great harbor of New York alone, where the Statue of Liberty beckons to every ship, twenty million immigrants have disembarked to become Americans. That monument bears an inscription which became known the world over wherever people longed to be free:

*. . . Give me your tired, your poor.*
*Your huddled masses yearning to be free.*
*The wretched refuse of your teeming shore.*
*Send these, the homeless, tempest-tossed to me.*
*I lift my lamp beside the golden door!*

The vast majority of those who came to America from other lands were not the elite of their societies. They were indeed the tired, the poor, the huddled masses longing to be free. They were the small farmers and businessmen, the artisans and the indentured workers who, because of poverty or oppression, were willing to face the hazards of the unknown on a continent which had not been settled or even explored. They came to make a new way of life in freedom for themselves and their families.

Even before we became a nation, settlers had pressed beyond the Appalachian Mountains. While the Founding Fathers were struggling with the text of the Constitution in 1787, the Continental Congress, aware of the western migration, enacted the Northwest Ordinance dealing with that vast territory which now makes up the states of Ohio, Michigan, Indiana, Illinois and Wisconsin, and part of Minnesota. That Ordinance provided for the organization of territories and their eventual admission as states to the Union. It banned slavery throughout the territory, encouraged free public education, and guaranteed religious freedom and trial by jury. And further south, colonists were moving into what became the slave states of Kentucky and Tennessee.

Each successive wave of migration, like the earliest ones, was motivated by the Biblical assertion, "Now faith is the substance of things hoped for, the evidence of things not seen." They crossed mountains and streams which were in their primeval condition. They farmed land which had never been plowed. They built homes and factories, cities and highways, railroads and all the other things which go to make modern life.

And no matter where the frontier was there were always among them at every outpost those who were driven to go farther into the unknown— driven not by man or the elements but by a burning desire to know what was beyond the mountain ranges, and to realize the potential of what they might find.

Many of the poor who came here struggled out of ghettos to a more favorable position in life for their children. But there are still more recent arrivals who have not yet been able to escape their sordid surroundings. What a breach of trust it is— as well as a betrayal of a commitment to our own ideals—whenever any of these people, because of their race, or color, or creed, find hostility here instead of hospitality, or are awarded not light and warmth from the "lamp beside the golden door" but a badge of inferiority for conditions they are powerless to change.

Those without color have found it comparatively easy to work their way out of the slums. But the colored, particularly the blacks—almost twenty million of them—have carried a cross throughout our history, not because of anything they could change but because of well-known reasons not flattering to the rest of us. The condition of these citizens presents one of our greatest national problems.

It is imperative to remember in all of our

actions that our nation has developed as a plural society composed of people of every racial origin on earth. Our ancestors were urged to come here to populate the country, to develop its resources, and to build its economy and its institutions. We have enshrined in our Constitution the principle that all men are created equal and have made everyone born or naturalized in the United States a citizen with all the privileges and immunities inherent in that status. We must realize that the only way we can have unity throughout the nation is to accord the full spectrum of Constitutional rights equally to everyone. There is no other way. The color of a man's skin or the religion he espouses must not be a factor in according him rights. Everyone is entitled to equal protection of the laws. Any other course is bound to create intense bitterness and, in the end, chaos.

To our present discomfiture, however, we have for centuries segregated certain groups from the mainstream of American life. Now that that exclusion has caught up with us, we do not know how to communicate with them, and in effect, while using the same words, we speak different languages. Our boast for years has been that we have developed the most affluent society in recorded history; yet, admittedly, millions of Americans go to bed hungry every night. This does not add up to affluence. It is, at best, a paradox. Here we are,

53

plagued with problems of unemployment, relief and frustration, while surrounded on every side with extravagance of all kinds.

The Supreme Court of the United States more and more has been compelled to focus its attention upon the rights of the poor and underprivileged in a free society. A prime function of government has always been, as it was first declared in the time of Hammurabi, "to protect the weak against the strong." Most Americans have social compassion for the underprivileged and the unfortunate. But what is also imperatively needed is a political conception of compassion. By that I mean an understanding and consideration for the economic and political rights of those who are oppressed by our society for reasons beyond their control. Such people, who are found primarily in the urban slums and depressed rural areas, are largely uneducated, unskilled in any craft or in any phase of business, poverty-stricken in every sense of the word—economically, politically and socially. They are also the victims of our technology and of the speed with which we have vaulted from a simple rural society to a gigantic urban society. The more sophisticated technology becomes, the deeper the uneducated and unskilled sink in the mire.

When the cotton-picking machine came into being only a few years ago, approximately 900,000 unschooled and untrained cotton pickers with families, aggregating between two-and-a-half and three million people, were thrown out of their livelihood in the Southern states alone. These figures do not include those in the important cotton-growing states of California and Arizona where similar displacements took place. Hundreds of thousands who lost the only employment they were capable of drifted into the cities with the desperate hope of finding a place in our industrial world; but it, too, was closed to them because of their lack of skills and the great advances in automation. Itinerant workers experienced the same frustration because of the recent development of mechanical pickers and harvesters for orchard and field crops. In the last thirty years, the farm population of the nation has decreased from 31 million to 10 million, and a large percentage of those forced out of living on the farms are today dependent on welfare in the cities.

This occasioned great suffering among large segments of our population, and the efforts of the government to relieve it invariably met with resistance from those who believe that our concern for the unfortunates should be limited to the poorhouse as Dickens depicted it in *Oliver Twist*. That was true of old-age pensions, social security, unemployment compensation, minimum wages, and even aid to the blind and totally disabled. All of these were resisted as "socialism," but are now discussed rationally in terms of adequate funding rather than political acceptability.

Recently, similar resistance has developed to what is compendiously called "welfare." Because of disjointed statutes, faulty administration, and abuse by some, all of the categories of aid to the unfortunate are lumped under that term, and welfare has acquired a somewhat sinister meaning. But it is not, of course, an evil word. Indeed the Preamble to the Constitution includes the general welfare as one of its objectives. Many functions of the government are undertaken with welfare in mind, for the benefit of different segments of society, but as a term of debasement it seems to apply only to assistance to the unfortunate. When hundreds of millions of dollars are given to bankrupt railroads, failing defense manufacturers, shipping interests and the like, the words "welfare" or "relief" are not used. Instead, such things are done to "strengthen the economy." Perhaps welfare to needy individuals can someday be discussed with the same particularity and with the same equanimity as subsidy to industry and other impersonal beneficiaries.

The same metamorphosis is occurring in the field of health and medical care. Only a very few years ago any proposal for medical assistance that called for governmental participation in the health of the public was denounced by vested interests as the work of the Devil. It was "Communism" in its purest form. But today we have Medicare and Medicaid, and the questions under review are primarily how and when aid can be extended to other groups whose ill health, caused by the inaccessibility of medical attention, is weakening our society.

In considering the problems of intolerence and neglect in a multiracial society, we must not close our eyes to the danger to the rights of all inherent in the denial of rights to the few. That danger is visible all around us, today as never before.

# VI

# NOT AN EASY FORM
# OF GOVERNMENT

GOVERNMENTS ARE ORGANISMS and, like all others, function for good or ill, depending on the soil and atmosphere in which they come into being. They grow and prosper or decay and die as do others according to their substance rather than their form. They have different nomenclatures, but it is the manner in which they function that characterizes them. There are many kinds of government in the world today—empires, monarchies, dictatorships, democracies, republics, both unitary and federal—but they all fall into two classifications: those which function under some variation of the democratic process; and those which are totalitarian in the sense that the nation is ruled by the will of either one individual or of a small oligarchy, without direction from the citizenry at large. Our government is dedicated to the democratic process, and is in form a federal republic which contemplates universal participation in its affairs: all citizens have certain rights and privileges on the one hand and corresponding duties and responsibilities on the other.

Though Englishmen live under a monarchy and Americans under a republican form; though we live under a written Constitution while Englishmen do not; though we have a separation of powers and they do not; and though they have a unitary system of government and we a federal system, still the people of both countries enjoy practically identical freedoms.

On the other hand, since our Constitution—the oldest in the world—was written, others have been conceived that follow ours quite closely. Yet, despite similar language, a number of these "democratic" constitutions are interpreted and administered so differently that it is difficult to believe they guarantee the same freedoms.

Perhaps the most dramatic example of different interpretations of similar constitutional language is to be found in the Russian and American constitutions. The Constitution of the U.S.S.R., adopted in 1936, and as amended in 1965, contains the following provisions:

*Article 125. In conformity with the interests of the working people, and in order to strengthen the Socialist system, the citizens of the U.S.S.R. are guaranteed by law; (a) freedom of speech; (b) freedom of the press; (c) freedom of assembly including the holding of mass meetings; (d) freedom of street expressions and demonstrations.*

*Article 124. In order to ensure to citizens freedom of conscience, the church in the U.S.S.R. is separated from the state, and the school from the church. Freedom of religious worship and freedom of antireligious propaganda is recognized for all citizens.*

*Article 127. Citizens of the U.S.S.R. are guaranteed inviolability of the person. No person shall be placed under arrest except by decision of a court of law or with the sanction of a procurator.*

*Article 122. Women in the U.S.S.R. are accorded all rights on an equal footing with men in all spheres of economic, government, culture, politics and other social activity.*

*Article 123. Equality of rights of citizens of the U.S.S.R., irrespective of their nationality or race in all spheres of economic, government, culture, politics and other social activity is an indefeasible law.*

How similar these sections are to our Bill of Rights, with its guarantees of freedom of speech, of the press, of association, of the right to petition the government, the right to be free from unreasonable searches and seizures. Yes, how similar these constitutional privileges are, but how different the quality and the reality of the life of the two peoples living under them.

The reason, of course, is apparent. In the U.S.S.R. the government is supreme and omnipresent in every respect, with the rights of individuals subordinated to it. The people have no way to enforce the language of their Constitution. Most of the declared freedoms are inaccessible to them.

In the United States the people are sovereign. The powers of the government are only those delegated to it by the people. The democratic process, by definition, is one in which "The supreme power is vested in the people and exercised by them or by their elected agents under a free electoral system."

The word "democracy" was given to us by

61

the Greeks—"demo" meaning people and "cracy" meaning form of government. It was the Greeks who first established city-states in accordance with the principle of government by the people. Athens started on its way toward a democracy under Solon, the great lawgiver, about 594 B.C., at a time when all the land and political power had been in the hands of the nobles. Solon abolished serfdom, divided the land, and placed additional governing power in the Assembly which he opened to all free men—the propertied class. He was interested in social justice, and, when asked how it could be achieved in Athens, he said, "We can have justice whenever those who have not been injured by injustice are as outraged by it as those who have been."

During and following Solon's time, city-states, governed by the people, sprang up in the Ionian Sea, and under the leadership of Athens were organized into the Delian League about 478 B.C. The League prospered, and within twenty-five years there were probably more than two hundred members. However, the city-states began fighting among themselves, and the people even grew weary of self-government. Athens then attempted to hold them together by force and, in doing so, became an Empire, only to be defeated militarily by Sparta in a short time, bringing an end to the league of city-states about 404 B.C. A few years later, in

378 B.C., an effort was made to restore the League, but in 338 B.C., after repeated military defeats at the hands of the Macedonians, it was finally destroyed. Athens then fell into the hands of successive conquerors and, having been sacked by Rome in 86 B.C., remained for centuries a small satellite city of the Roman Empire, its short-lived experiment with democracy and the elements of a republic crushed.

Rome, which succeeded the power of Athens, was never a pure democracy. It experimented with the democratic process and with the fundamentals of a republic, but it never placed the power of government in the people themselves. Its beginning is shrouded by antiquity, but as far as we know it began as a patrician aristocracy about 753 B.C. In 500 B.C. the Roman Empire was created with a modicum of local governmental responsibility in the citizenship which later evolved to include all free men in the Empire. The Empire survived a thousand years, until A.D. 476 when, after the government became corrupt and citizenship debased, Rome fell to the Goths.

Along with the demise of the Roman Empire went the literature, most of the culture and the Roman concept of law. The first few centuries following were commonly called the Dark Ages, but more recently it has been recognized that there remained from the Empire at least a ray of light.

By A.D. 1000 the feudal system had become almost universal in Europe, but as more power accrued to the emerging commercial cities, feudalism was supplanted by the absolute monarchies of Europe based on the concept of the Divine Right of Kings.

This period, however, was accompanied by continuing pressure for the transfer of more political power to the people. It fostered the rich development of European civilization, marking the transition from medieval to modern times. It was, indeed, a Renaissance, as the period was called—a time of brilliant accomplishments in education, and particularly in literature, as well as the sciences and the arts. It was also an age of discovery and exploration—Columbus discovered America in 1492—and of an economic revolution.

In the seventeenth century America was colonized by the English, and the seeds of our own democracy were planted. Along with great scientific advances, and the study of life and law and human institutions, there developed a group of European philosophers who did much to determine the course of history. These men characterized what has come to be known as the Age of Enlightenment or the Age of Reason. Benjamin Franklin and Thomas Jefferson were especially familiar with and disciples of their philosophies.

The unique beliefs of the members of our Constitutional Convention, who both hated and

64

feared concentrated power, led them inexorably to the creation of a federal republic, which was nonexistent in the world at that time. A federal republic is neither a simple form of government nor, as we have noted, an easy one to live under. Indeed, it is perhaps the most complex of modern governmental organizations. Even more important, it imposes greater responsibilities on the citizenry than any other.

Our Founding Fathers contemplated two distinct levels of constitutional government—national and state. The United States Constitution makes provision for those governmental requirements which affect the entire nation, while state constitutions cover matters affecting only life within the state.

There is one major difference between the two—that difference is to be found in the so-called Supremacy Clause of the Sixth Article of the United States Constitution, which reads as follows:

*This Constitution, and the Laws of the United States which shall be made in Pursuance thereof; and all Treaties made, or which shall be made, under the Authority of the United States, shall be the supreme Law of the Land; and the Judges in every State shall be bound thereby, any Thing in the Constitution or Laws of any State to the Contrary notwithstanding.*

65

Similarity among all state constitutions stems from the fact that Article IV of the Constitution provides—

*The United States shall guarantee to every State of the Union a Republican form of Government. . . .*

This means that on admission into the Union, a state must first present its constitution to the Congress for approval. Every state constitution, like the federal Constitution, calls for a division of powers among the legislative, executive and judicial branches of the government. However, aside from such constitutional division of powers, rather substantial differences exist in the various state constitutions because, subject only to the federal requirement for a republican form of government, the states have complete autonomy in the establishment of their relationship with their component parts—their cities, counties, school boards, courts and commissions.*

---

* Actually, in all but one of the states, these differences are of little significance because all of them have evolved from the common law of England. Louisiana is significantly different because it was once a French-Spanish possession and had its roots in the civil law of Rome. However, its constitution, although based upon that system of law for its local government, adapted itself to a republican form of government to the satisfaction of the Congress of the United States. Having provided for a representative form of government with a separation of powers, it satisfied the federal requirements as to matters within its jurisdiction, and permitted the local civil law autonomy contemplated in our federal system.

Our government grows in complexity just as our society does. There are rarely sharp lines between that which is the province of government and that which is private. Private problems, long left unattended and hence grown large over the years, become problems for government. Except for special provinces such as foreign affairs, it is hard to think of any government activity that did not have its roots in the inability of local neighborhoods or communities to solve a problem that affected more than one of its citizens. In such an interdependent setting, each has his own part to play and each has his own sphere of influence. There is no one so poor or so oppressed that his life, for good or ill, cannot affect others.

Even two centuries ago, in our simple agrarian society of less than four million people, New York was our largest city. But it had a population of only 33,000. The problems of the environment, poverty, education, employment, health and crime were in concept local responsibilities.

With the industrial revolution came the influx of foreign labor by the millions, the exploitation of our natural resources, the dehumanizing influence of the machine.

Throughout this transformation, our business and industrial life expanded beyond local and state lines to the point where their complexities called for both federal regulation and financial help.

Government at all levels grew in size with the problems. Today the functions of local, state and national government are so intertwined that only research and budgetary accounting can determine the true relationship between them. In the federal government alone, there are approximately three million civilian officers and employees. In state and local governments, the number is almost ten million (9,216,000). Many people, I am sure, believe that this is an inordinate number, and that better planning and administration could eliminate many of them. In some agencies, that might well be true. But only constant attention by the citizenry, at the polls and through community activities designed to prevent unnecessary expansion, can keep needless growth within reasonable bounds; bureaucracy, unwatched, has a natural tendency to expand.*

The activities of the mass of public servants are so manifold and so interwoven with the normal activities of the people that we can hardly move without encountering government in some form or other. Of course, a sizable number relate to services as in any business. But there are many thousands of policy-making opportunities. It is honorable em-

---

* As evidence of this, the entire budget of the federal government at the turn of the century, including expenditures for defense, was $520,-861,000, and the entire cost of local and state governments at that time was $1,095,000,000 for all the states of the Union. Today our federal budget aggregates $200 billion with about $80 billion for defense alone.

ployment and, in these days, when an effort is being made to equalize Civil Service salaries with those in private employment, citizens are increasingly willing to dedicate themselves to the public service.

The size of our nation—its enormous population, the vast machinery of our government, the intricacies of the economy, the mechanization of industry with mass production procedures—has a tendency to befog many people and to leave them with a sense of unimportance, of futility in making their actions as citizens meaningful.

This is understandable but unfortunate. The fact is that the size of our nation has been a great boon to us. If it had been "Balkanized" as was Central Europe or as the developing nations of Africa and Asia appear to have been, we might have fallen prey to stronger powers. Instead of freedom of commerce and travel from the Atlantic to the Pacific, we would have border checks every few hundred miles, with Iron Curtains to keep our people separated and at odds with one another.

No nation or individual can escape the force of history. If we were not one nation, we would have a disjointed continent. We might have lost the freedoms, the enterprise, and the vision we have cherished since the colonists landed at Jamestown in 1607. No matter how we might have allowed ourselves to be divided, or what other system of government we might have adopted, the nation would still be governed by people, and the basic question would remain: "By one, a few, many, or all?"

Every generation in our history has created a backlog of problems, particularly those generations which have experienced great change. But no generation in recorded history has brought about as much change as ours. As a result, we have had to cope with more problems than preceding generations. Life has indeed become extremely complicated compared with that of the colonists at the time of the American Revolution or even at the time the oldest among us were born. I know that has been true during my own lifetime. When I was a boy living in a small town, life was quite simple, and government touched us very little.

We now have a fast-growing population of over two hundred million people, and a gross national product of a trillion dollars. The less moving space we have, the more we have to make sure that although we have freedom it will be the kind of freedom in which one person following his own desires does not injure another.

Is the structure of our society complete? The answer, of course, is no. Much progress has been made, as much as can be claimed by any nation on earth. But we have made mistakes, and have often needed to rebuild faulty construction.

I believe that those mistakes (and future ones) can be remedied and the structure completed in keeping with the original design. This can be done through a rededication to that design which recognized that the essential ingredient of our system is the co-existence of order and liberty.

Is such a coexistence possible? No one knows for sure; many countries have tried and failed. We do know that the compatibility of order and liberty must be relearned and re-earned by each generation. It is a union based on experience, not abstract logic. But we in the United States have a great advantage over most people. Our Constitution provides a basic framework which provides for order and liberty. It allows the majority of the people to make economic, social and political decisions about life in America which are binding on everyone. At the same time, it protects important individual rights absolutely. No majority can, for example, decide to prohibit a certain religion or deny a particular man a jury trial, or arbitrarily order that his house be searched without cause. Another way of stating the same thing is to say that the people who ratified the Constitution and the Bill of Rights gave a limited grant of power to the government—enough to achieve order, but not enough to destroy liberty.

To state that the Constitution makes the compatibility of order and liberty possible is one thing;

to ensure that both ingredients are protected is another. The balance is delicate. It puts to the test Benjamin Franklin's warning that to create a republic is one thing, to maintain it another.

Our nation is an organism as much as is the human body. It has functional parts—trade, commerce, business, labor, contented homes and wholesome neighborhoods—which are as vital to it as the heart, lungs, kidneys and liver. It has arteries—highways, railways, rivers, bays, ships, telephone, radio, television—which must remain as open for business, transportation and communication as the arteries of the body that lead to the heart. It has veins which reach every minute part of the body in the form of education, cultural and social activities. It has emotions, of joy, anger, concern, apathy, frustration and motivation, as does the individual. It has moving parts which are as important as the arms, the legs, the eyes and the ears; these are the agencies of government—city, county, state and nation. It has a soul which can be lost by greed, intolerance, ignorance, corruption or indifference.

These similarities between the body politic and the human body demonstrate that the proper functioning of all parts is as important in one as the other. Neither can be wholly healthy if any part is diseased. A city, sick with slums, ghettos, crime, corruption and poverty can be as dangerous to the nation as a damaged heart, a palsied arm or a contagious disease to the individual. It is, therefore, essential that we, as responsible citizens, concern ourselves at all times with the economic, political and moral health of every segment of our society. There is so much that each of us can do to help.

If we, for example, had given greater attention to the conservation of our natural resources as we developed the country, we would not have ecological problems of the magnitude we face today. If we had been more conscious of human values, we would not have the problems of poverty, city blight, degradation and crime which now confront us in such virulent form. If we had not isolated ourselves from the rest of the world and its problems for so long, we would be much farther along in outlawing war as a means of settling disputes.

All of these problems now press upon us in gigantic form. Only an aroused citizenry can ensure remedial action. We alone can provide the leverage, the necessary power to fulfill the vision of unity and peace implicit in the Constitution.

# VII

## THE CITIZEN AND
## PUBLIC LIFE

WHEN I WAS a little fellow growing up in a small railroad town of a few hundred people in the great Central Valley of California—then semiarid and dotted with only a few farming and railroad towns—one of the few cultural activities was the annual series of Chautauqua Lectures. My father always took me to hear them, and one particularly has remained with me through life.

It was delivered by Reverend Russell H. Conwell, and it was entitled "Acres of Diamonds." Reverend Conwell was journeying down the Tigris River in the land of the ancient Assyrians when he was told a story of India by his boatman guide:

*He said there once lived not far from the River Indus an ancient Persian by the name of Al Hafed. He said that Al Hafed owned a very large farm with orchards, grain fields and gardens. He was a contented and wealthy man—contented because he was wealthy, and wealthy because he was contented. One day there visited this old farmer one of those ancient Buddhist priests. . . . And the old priest told Al Hafed that if he had a handful of diamonds he could purchase a whole county, and with a mine of diamonds he could place his children upon thrones through the influence of their great wealth. Al Hafed heard all about diamonds and how much they were worth, and went to his bed that night a poor man—not that he had lost anything, but poor because he was discontented and discontented because he was poor. He said: "I want a mine of diamonds!" So he lay awake all night, and early in the morning sought out the priest. . . . He awoke that priest out of his dreams and said to him, "Will you tell me where I can find diamonds? I want to be immensely rich," said Al Hafed, "but I don't know where to go." "Well," said the priest, "if you will find a river that runs over white sand between high mountains, in those sands you will always see diamonds" . . . . So he sold his farm, collected his money at interest, left his family in charge of a neighbor, and away he went in search of diamonds.*

75

*He began very properly, to my mind, at the Mountains of the Moon. Afterwards he went around into Palestine, then wandered on into Europe, and at last, when his money was all spent, and he was in rags, wretchedness and poverty, he stood on the shore of that bay in Barcelona, Spain, when a tidal wave came rolling in through the Pillars of Hercules and the poor, afflicted, suffering man could not resist the awful temptation to cast himself into that incoming tide, and he sank beneath its foaming crest, never to rise in this life again.*

Then Reverend Conwell told us how one day Al Hafed's successor took his camel out to the garden to drink, and discovered a black stone having "an eye of light." The old priest saw the stone and immediately recognized it as a diamond.

*Then together they rushed to the garden and stirred up the white sands with their fingers and found others more beautiful, more valuable diamonds than the first, and thus, said the guide to me, were discovered the diamond mines of Golconda, the most magnificent diamond mines in all the history of mankind. . . . [Then] he said that had Al Hafed remained at home and dug in his own cellar, or in his own garden, instead of wretchedness, starvation, poverty and death in a strange land, he would have had "acres of diamonds"—for every*

*acre, yes, every shovelful of that old farm after-*
*wards revealed the gems which since have dec-*
*orated the crowns of monarchs.*

When I heard the lecture (it was around the
turn of the century) the moral of the story—that
we often overlook challenges and opportunities
close at home for the exaggerated promise of
things far away—was not lost on me.*

There is no question that we have been less
than diligent in recognizing important opportunities all about us, and often in being too prodigal
with those we have found. Undoubtedly, had our
land been less abundant—and our urge to "Go
West, young man, go West," less strong—we would
have used our resources more providently, and
would have preserved them more faithfully for
future generations. Instead with an easy come, easy
go approach, we exploited them indiscriminately,
bringing about erosion of hillsides and pollution
of streams, rivers, lakes, bays, the ocean itself,
destroying animal and marine life and dangerously
contaminating the air we breathe.

We are at last awakening to the necessity of

---

* Dr. Conwell himself lived by the lesson of his lecture. He used the
proceeds to educate poor boys and to establish a university in his home
city which he lived to see train 100,000 students who otherwise would
have been deprived of an education. The school, Temple University of
Philadelphia, is now a distinguished center of learning for 26,288
students.

protecting the environment in which we must live. Until recently the small band of conservationists who were sounding the alarm were considered visionaries or radicals. Now they are being listened to by all branches of the government, and candidates for public office are vying with each other to propose programs for dealing with pollution and other environmental hazards.

In many areas of public concern, a few determined citizens have finally converted a multitude. It is the American way of solving problems— slow and tedious at times, but often satisfyingly effective. So it behooves us not to be fainthearted when we are not with the majority. No one can be active in all of the causes generated in our country, but everyone can participate in at least one. Because our government is representative in character, i.e., representative of the people, some of our citizens must be willing to submit themselves for election to the various governmental offices or to otherwise pursue a governmental career. There is an old political saw to the effect that "The office should seek the man, not the man seek the office." But this is not based upon either logic or wisdom. The man who does not seek the office is rarely, if ever, elected, and that is as it should be. The man who holds public office should want the position; he should train himself for it; he should

78

know the potentialities of the office and what its jurisdictional limits are, as well as the problems he will be called upon to solve if he achieves it. He should analyze himself to make sure that he has the prerequisites and the motivation for the job he seeks, the independence to serve according to his own conscience unaffected by bias or prejudice or conflict of interest, and a willingness to subject his conduct to the scrutiny of his fellow citizens.

Soul searching by candidates may not always enable them to evaluate correctly their susceptibility to bias or prejudice since certain social patterns are often conducive to inborn prejudices. But there can be no justification for their misjudging or concealing a conflict of interest. Every public official or prospective officeholder can tell when his personal interest, be it financial or otherwise, conflicts with the public interest which he has professed to represent. He knows that no man can serve two masters, and that when personal interest conflicts with public interest, invariably the latter suffers.

Nevertheless, conflict of interest has become so common that it is disregarded by many officeholders and is so seldom disclosed to the citizenry that it rarely attracts public attention. It is, however, the most demoralizing influence in government at each level and threatens the integrity of our institutions. Every official should avoid it as

79

he would the plague, and every citizen should scrutinize the public service to detect its destructive influence.

From this point of view, elective office is an honorable calling and can be productive of lasting satisfactions. To be entrusted by the votes of the people with authority to represent them in important affairs of government is a privilege which comes to comparatively few people, particularly in the federal government, where there are but two national elective offices—the Presidency and the Vice-Presidency. There are, of course, the members of Congress to be elected, but each citizen is limited to voting for the two Senatorial positions of his state and for one member of the House of Representatives from the district in which he resides. There are 435 such districts as equal in size according to population as they can practically be made.

The importance of these offices to everyone in the United States is immeasurable, and the responsibility of every citizen to vote for the candidate of his choice is a significant one. The offices are usually hotly contested, and frequently the outcome depends on a very few votes. There have been instances when a change of only a few thousand votes would have elected a different President and Vice-President. Many contests for the United States Senate and the House of Representatives have been decided by a handful of votes. When former President Johnson was first elected to the Senate from Texas—then the largest state in the Union—he won his primary election by eighty-seven votes. If only forty-four of these voters had cast their ballots for his opponent, he would not have been nominated to run, and thus might have been deprived of the opportunity for the distinguished public career which eventually brought him to the attention of all of the American people. In all probability, he never would have been President of the United States.

In the 1970 elections, there were a number of Senatorial and Congressional seats so closely contested that it took days for election officers to determine who should be declared the winners. And some of the tallies were close enough to require expensive and time-consuming recounts.

Some years ago in the State of California, in a primary campaign for Congress, two candidates tied. Neither candidate cared to assume the financial burden of a recount and left the decision to be made according to the law, which in this case was by lot. The candidates drew straws and thus the State of California sent to the Congress a Representative chosen by chance rather than by a majority of the people. Significantly, at least 50 percent of those qualified to vote in that election did not do so. If any one of that group had voted, his

81

vote would have determined who the Congressman would be.

One can never tell what the value of his vote will be. It might be merely one of a definite majority or minority. On the other hand, it might determine the outcome. If we look at state elections involving governors, legislators, state, county, city and district governments, we find the likelihood of inconclusive majorities increasingly greater in proportion to the diminished size of the voting constituency. Each of these elective positions plays some part in the governmental scheme, and many of them have policy-making functions which greatly affect our way of life.

Candidates alone do not make a meaningful election. They represent only the tip of the iceberg. In every election, there are issues to be defined, solutions to be proposed, qualifications to be appraised, and possible results envisioned. Often, when a political leader proposes a solution to a public problem, the idea is not original with him but is rather his reaction to a public need as reflected through public opinion. In other words, he is following what he considers to be the will of the people. This thought was dramatically expressed in the story concerning one of the leaders in the French Revolution. He was conversing with a friend at a street corner when a large crowd of marching people passed them. He quickly excused himself from his friend, saying, "Those are my followers. I must lead them," and he ran to catch up with them.

So it is in American life today. The people are often in advance of their leaders. This is consistent with the realities of the present and with the American tradition. Men and women elected or appointed to public office are like people in other walks of life. They are not all self-starters or scholars; they might not even be diligent in their duties. Some, once in office, are complacent and satisfied with conditions contrary to the public welfare so long as there is no public outcry. And in these days of promiscuous poll-taking, many are moved to act only when the publicly reported polls demonstrate concern by a majority of the people. Others are subservient to powerful vested interests whose only aim is to strengthen their dominant positions. Still others are anxious to attack problems, but cannot see enough public support to encourage them in their efforts. Many of our serious problems are not attacked until they reach the crisis stage, and then it may be too late to achieve maximum results.

It is also in the spirit of our institutions for the people to lead in governmental affairs. Our nation would never have come into being had they not done so two hundred years ago. The Founding Fathers labored for months in the Constitutional

Convention to diffuse power and to leave as much of it as possible to the people. While they provided us with a representative form of government, they expected the people always to be in control.

Tom Paine, a militant American Revolutionist, said, "Give us a lever and we shall move the world." In our system, the people are the lever, and with the power they can muster almost anything can be accomplished. Even modest citizens, with faith in our institutions and faith in themselves, can do much to create an atmosphere hospitable to the good life originally envisioned for our nation. Outside of politics a citizen, pursuing a quiet and unassuming life, can contribute in many ways to the happiness of his neighborhood, his city, his state and his nation. It would be wrong, of course, to tell another how or to what extent he should participate in his government. While the right to participate is the right to do so publicly, the exercise of the right can be as private as any citizen chooses to make it. To suggest that everyone should be interested in holding public office or in working for the government would be the height of absurdity; to suggest that everyone should actively participate in election campaigns would likewise be ludicrous.

Human nature is of such multiform character and man's experiences in life are so diverse that no identical patterns are apparent even for any two people. Some are outgoing and gregarious; others are retiring and self-contained. Some are articulate; others are more contemplative. Some are philosophers; others activists. Some are physically dynamic; others phlegmatic.

But inasmuch as our Constitution endows all citizens with the right to participate in their government, it would seem that, at the very least, everyone should be willing to inform himself of the issues and personalities which affect the governments of which he is a part and, in his all-important responsibility to vote, to share with his fellow citizens the benefit of his considered thought. We cannot delegate to our governmental representatives the full responsibility for protection of our freedoms from erosion. Such protection can be had only through an understanding on the part of each citizen of what our freedoms are, how and why they came into being and the degree to which their spirit dominates our institutions and the life of our country.

# VIII

## EDUCATING FOR CITIZENSHIP

INTEREST IN PUBLIC AFFAIRS is something that should be acquired early in life, the sooner the better because in this field of human activity, like all others, the parade moves along, and after it has once passed there is little opportunity to catch up with it. When I was Governor of California, I knew many successful men whose age had compelled them to retire. They were men of means who had made their mark in the business world because of single-minded devotion to their work. They had no time for public affairs, nor any particular interest in them. But upon retirement, they felt a lonesomeness stemming from a lack of belonging, and real-

86

ized, perhaps for the first time, that the money they had acquired during their business lives did not bring sufficient satisfaction to their retirement years.

A number of these men came to me to inquire if I could find jobs in the state government that would help them to shed the feeling of uselessness which had suddenly possessed them. They would say, "Governor, I do not care about the money involved; I am only interested in being active. I do not care what kind of a job it is—anything to keep me busy."

These were honest men, able men, but they did not really mean that any work would satisfy them. What was implicit in each of their requests was: an office, properly equipped; a meaningful function to perform; and a staff to be supervised. I had a deep sympathy for them and tried my best to find positions they could fill but to my regret, and theirs, I was unable to because they had no concept of public service, its problems or its needs. Public office, like any other important endeavor, is a distinct business which can only be handled effectively by people who are experienced and informed as well as motivated to do a thorough job.

There are two important aspects of man's nature. First, he is a social being and has a societal relationship with all others in his society. He cannot live entirely unto himself. Second, he is a

87

political entity and has a relationship with the institutions under which he lives as well as with his fellow citizens. He cannot escape either relationship. The only question is what those relationships are to be. The two aspects are not antithetical; in fact, they sometimes merge in a manner that defies disentanglement. Yet they are distinct sides of man's nature. Both call for lifetime preparation, and for the acquisition of knowledge from the same sources—the family, school, friends, group association, church and political affiliation. The rudiments of both are available in the home before outside associations are material. It is there that the child first becomes conscious of affection for those who provide him with food, shelter and protection from bodily harm. There he becomes conscious of the need to adjust his ways to the ways of others. The child who does not learn before going to school that there is authority which he must respect, and that his way of life must recognize the need for honesty and fairness in dealing with others, starts life with a severe handicap. Some overcome that handicap, but too many others carry it as a scar through life.

The schools can nurture such proper sentiments, but they have neither the time nor opportunity to inculcate them in children who have not first learned them at home. For example, the child learns even before going to school that the policeman on the beat is there to help people who need it, not just to arrest people for doing wrong. I remember when my own children were little. We would take them to the school corner where there was a large uniformed traffic policeman. All the little ones from the neighborhood would stand on the sidewalk awaiting his signal to cross. They would not step off the curb, but would call, "Dan! Dan!" until he turned, smiled, took a few steps toward them, and waved them across. Then they would run toward him and across the street to school, admiring him and saying a few cheery words as they scampered.

I always conjured on this wonderful relationship between citizens, young as they were, and officers of the law. And it made it easier for our children to understand, when we told them that if they ever needed help to look for a policeman and tell their problems to him. Most policemen spend a major part of their time doing helpful things for people, many of whom they do not know and have probably never seen before. There isn't a better way to inspire order in the community.

Children normally first become acquainted with community life in our schools. They learn that there are rules for school attendance; that there are rules for order in the classroom; that there is authority in the teacher and superior authority in the principal. Their studies are assigned to them, and

they are graded on both their academic achievements and their deportment. All of these things are
designed to impart a sense of belonging, a recognition of order, and an inspiration for achievement.
They involve advancement both as a social being
and as a political entity. However, in too many
schools, children in the elementary grades are
taught hardly anything concerning government,
and they come to little or no appreciation of democratic values except those they might have learned
in their own homes. Moreover, in civics and government courses in the high schools, students are
sometimes taught little more than the mechanics by
which mayors, city councils, governors, legislators,
the President, Vice-President, Senators and Congressmen are qualified and elected to office. The
basic freedoms are neglected, and, as investigators
have found, a large percentage of high school students have no understanding of American freedoms, how they came into being, and why and how
they must be protected.

Research in this field appears to have been
desultory and sporadic, but some of it has been
assembled in compact form in a pamphlet on secondary schools issued by the National Educational
Association through its National Council for the
Social Studies. Entitled "Political Socialization of
American Youth," it points out that in two university towns—one in the South, the other in the

North—between 95 and 98 percent of the registered voters were in agreement with statements such as "Democracy is the best form of Government," and "Every citizen should have an equal chance to influence Government policy," and "People in the minority should be free to try to win majority support for their opinions."

But many of these same people who showed support for these general principles were not willing to implement them: 79 percent of them said that only taxpayers should be allowed to vote to decide the merits of a tax-supported project. The right to give an antireligious speech was rejected by about one third, and two fifths of those in the Southern city and one third in the Northern city agreed with the statement, "A Negro should not be allowed to run for Mayor in this city." This is typical of what we so often hear in politics: "I agree with the principle of the proposal, but I am opposed to the suggested remedy."

How often have we seen elected officials avoid responsibility in some manner? An elderly state senator once told me that in his district there was a little town so dead that the people had nothing to argue about except whether or not they should have a new church. But that issue was so controversial that it kept the town in an uproar. Everybody took sides and fought bitterly over it. One old gentleman, though, rode through all the acrimony without it ever touching him. For years he was chairman of the Board of Deacons, but finally decided to retire, asking the church to put his son in his place. This was done. In a very short time the son was right in the midst of the fight over the new church. His store was boycotted; his wife was banned from the church socials; and the schoolchildren threw rocks at his children. Unable to stand it any longer, he went to his father and said, "Dad, I am in great trouble. You got me into it, and you must get me out of it," and he told of what was happening to him and his family. The old gentleman heard him out and then finally said, "My boy, don't worry. I will tell you how to avoid all those difficulties. In the future, whenever there is a proposal for a new church, you vote for the new church but never vote for a site. No matter what site is proposed, you vote against it, and your troubles will be over."

Issues must be confronted, studied, debated and decided according to their merits. Our schools can be most influential in forming and guiding attitudes, conceptions and beliefs about citizenship and the operation of our political system. It is unfortunate that frequently so narrow an approach to responsible citizenship is made in so many schools. A just criticism would appear to be that in some communities, because of the pressure of local public opinion, teachers are fearful of opening their classes to the discussion of important and even controversial public issues that might lead their pupils to think problems through to conclusions even though they might be inimical to local beliefs. As a result, civics and government classes are watered down to discussion of government tables of organization and stereotyped questions that suggest "acceptable" answers. The NCSS pamphlet points out:

*By pouring civic information and historical knowledge into students, instead of teaching them how to think and analyze social problems, our educational system misses its great opportunity.*

In conclusion, it suggests that

*. . . central to the improvement of political socialization strategies of secondary schools should be efforts to keep the socialization process open-ended by providing young people with the tools to think reflectively about their beliefs, with disposition to examine critically traditional practices, and with an educational atmosphere conducive to reflective thinking. This approach to improve political socialization through formal instruction would involve a revision of current civics and government courses to bring them into line with current scholarship. It would involve discarding many American*

93

*myths that are taught as facts in typical civics and government courses, and that may be dysfunctional in the real political world. It would involve teaching students skills of reflective thinking. It would involve creating an academic environment conducive to creativity, free expression, inquiry, and open-mindedness. It would involve giving high school youth considerable opportunities for meaningful decision-making.*

How important this advice is when our young people are confronted with the responsibility of voting at eighteen years of age. There are eleven million young people between eighteen and twenty-one. The significance of their voting responsibility is pointed up by the fact that in 1968 President Nixon was elected by a plurality—not a majority—of about 500,000 votes, and President Kennedy by half that number.

The stimulation of free thinking through the presentation of facts, views and arguments is essential to meaningful voting, or, in fact, any participation in governmental affairs. The citizen should be able to recognize the distinction between facts and opinion. In everyday usage this means the difference between news and propaganda. The basis from which we reason in public affairs is usually one or both of these sources of information.

News is defined as "information about recent

94

events of general interest as reported by news-papers, periodicals, radio or television"; and propa-ganda, as "dissemination of ideas, information, or rumor for the purpose of helping or injuring an institution, a cause, or a person." Both are essential to balanced reasoning, but one should be able to distinguish between the two. Some propaganda is good; some is bad. One should not be willing to be guided by either unless he knows the facts upon which it is based, in order that he might form an independent judgment. The news as published by responsible news agencies in our country is as factual as any information available to us. But the news agencies also, in a sense, carry propa-ganda items in the form of editorial and personal columns, as do radio and television. These are good, if one reads or listens to a cross section of them, but they should be taken for what they are —opinion, not fact. Where the citizen is able to distinguish between fact and opinion he can then, through his own reasoning, arrive at his own in-dependent conclusion.

There are today so many ways that one can make oneself more knowledgeable. The news of the day on radio and television and in the press is available to everyone. There are magazines in al-most every field of thought on newsstands or in public libraries. And in libraries are books on almost every subject with librarians to help one locate them for the asking. Most communities have neighborhood groups for the discussion of local affairs. There are party organizations for the discussion of political problems. There are public mass meetings for the same purpose. There are labor unions and business associations. There are adult educational activities in most school systems and many colleges and universities. There are art museums and community cultural activities which broaden the mind and mellow the outlook toward one's fellow human beings and the environment. Most of these services are free and are open to exploration limited only by one's desire to use them. All expand the vision and the activities that add up to responsible citizenship.

# IX

## CRIME, VIOLENCE AND DISSENT

IF THERE IS one situation more responsible than others for the tensions and divisiveness in our society today, it is undoubtedly the war atmosphere in which we have existed for several decades. War is always demoralizing and leaves in its wake a lowering of moral standards. People under forty have had to live under the influence of some kind of war for most of their lives. During all these years, the youth of our country has been uprooted from normal life. Tens of millions of our fine young men have been taken into the armed forces, most of them stationed in distant parts of the world, uncertain of their future and with home ties loosened.

Yet at home, their elders—or at least a majority of them—have been enjoying an affluence unknown in prior years or generations.

On their return to civilian life, after risking their lives for their country, our young soldiers have quickly seen through the materiality of the age, and have begun to question the professed values of society. They, and others of their generation, see from their vantage point that major problems of American life are not being forthrightly challenged, and are being piled one upon the other for their generation to deal with in the indefinite future.

They are seeking new values and new solutions. Sometimes bizarre methods have been tried —even destructive ones—because these youngsters are in a hurry. And often they are anxious to get rid of old methods before they have found new ones.

The generation gap must be closed, and cooperation restored. We cannot insist all is well because both young and old know this is not so. Nor can we "burn down the house to roast the pig," as an old saying goes. There is much the older generation would keep. There is much youth would change. Somewhere between, a line can be drawn to satisfy the needs of both. We are all mothers and fathers or sons and daughters. Basically, we have similar ideals and the affection of kinship. Surely, there is common ground on which all can meet.

First, we must work our way to peace both abroad and at home, recognizing that we cannot expect our young people to be peaceable and humanitarian at home while we go on conscripting them and teaching them to kill abroad. Nonetheless, our citizens are sufficiently aware of the possibility of a nuclear holocaust to see that we must remain strong enough to ward off the danger of any such destruction until that happy day arrives when the nations of the world will outlaw war as a means of settling international disputes. The possible danger from outside our borders is so apparent that it cannot escape the attention of any American.

On the other hand, the internal danger of erosion of our freedoms is likewise with us, but not so apparent. We know that the constant dripping of water can wear away stone, and that even the gentle rain can quickly erode the side of a mountain that does not have protective foliage. And so our freedoms—the finest products of civilization—can be eroded, a little here and a little there, until they become honored more in the breach than in the observance.

World history is replete with illustrations of such erosion and the resulting tyranny. The constant repetition of such blackouts of freedom makes meaningful the adage I've mentioned before that those who fail to learn the lessons of history are doomed to repeat them.

For many years the crime problem in America has grown until it is now intolerable; yet the growth of slums and the deterioration of our cities where most crime is spawned have proceeded unabated. Cumbersome and obsolete court procedures still prevail and congestion is the rule rather than the exception in most metropolitan areas. Many police departments are understaffed, ill-trained and underpaid in spite of their important responsibilities.

Today, there is so much crime in the world, and particularly in the United States, that our citizens are justifiably restive in demanding that better methods be used to prevent it. This condition must be remedied. It is a gigantic job, and to do it effectively will take the combined efforts of every branch of the government on all levels, with the cooperation of all good citizens. In assessing our joint task, there is a great need for introspection on the part of all of us because, to some extent at least, we are all responsible for the conditions which breed crime. It is, therefore, proper to put under the searchlight of public scrutiny not only public agencies but the extent to which the public itself cooperates or fails to do so in the enforcement of the law. It serves no useful purpose to search for scapegoats. There are too many facets to the problem, and the underlying causes for the high rate of crime are too pervasive in our society to justify fixing responsibility on any agency of government, or on any one segment of society.

To have an ordered society, free from crime, we must have order and wholesomeness in the home, in the neighborhood, on the streets, in business, and in government, together with dedication on the part of the citizenry to respect and revere the law.

Abraham Lincoln, always compassionate and understanding, expressed his concept of the law in these words:

*Let every American, every lover of liberty, every well-wisher to his posterity, swear by the blood of the Revolution never to violate in the least particular the laws of the country, and never to tolerate their violence by others. . . . Let reverence for the laws be breathed by every American mother to the lisping babe that prattles on her lap; let it be taught in schools, seminaries, and in colleges; let it be written in primers, spelling books, and in almanacs; let it be preached from the pulpit, proclaimed in legislative halls, and enforced in courts of justice. And, in short, let it become the political religion of the nation.*

To some this may sound simplistic or, perhaps, gushing with emotion. But if we are to have a diminution of crime in our day, we must resort to simple logic, human compassion and community spirit.

A nation which does not protect itself and its people against serious crime is, of course, failing in its most important obligation. But a nation which enforces its laws while violating the fundamental rights guaranteed to its citizens is contributing to its own ultimate destruction. We must have vigorous enforcement of the law, but that enforcement must be fair, equal in its application, and in accordance with our time-honored and loudly professed freedoms. In all facets of law enforcement— arrest, trial, conviction, punishment—officers and citizens must, in conscience, take to heart and try to understand the sordid conditions which breed the vast majority of crimes. We must, in effect, admonish ourselves as did John Bradford when he saw some poor wretch being taken to the place of execution: "But for the grace of God there goes John Bradford."

As essential as obedience to the law is, it affects only a minimal portion of our lives. Human relations are so complex that lawmakers cannot conceive everything needed to regulate human conduct. They can only enact the obvious. The more subtle and finer decisions of people must come from the moral judgments they make every time they come in contact with each other. This is the product of civilization built into our consciousness through the experiences of humankind since before recorded history. It determines conduct more, by far, than the law itself.

One need not be satisfied with all present conditions; in fact, it is undesirable to have such an attitude because there are always things which need correction. But one must be a "doer of things" to play one's part. To dissent from the status quo whenever and wherever he desires, is every man's privilege. His contribution, however, should never be judged solely by that dissent, but rather by what he does to help correct the evils of his time.

Where everyone is in favor of something, it takes no particular strength of character to go along with it. But to oppose the status quo for a good cause, facing the barbs of the majority, takes fortitude. And when diligently pursued through the years such opposition is a builder of character. Devotion to a good cause must bring one into contact with others, and ideas shared are the essence of a viable democracy.

Thus we see that the individual can be effective in our gargantuan society even though he may belong to a small minority at the beginning. For instance, the good citizen, when he disagrees with the law, does not defy it. He dissents from it and strives to change it. He may speak publicly and even stridently if it is necessary to be heard. He may propagandize with his neighbors and friends. He may lobby the state legislature or Congress as the situation demands, and in like manner he may appeal to his governor or his President. He may associate himself with others, and work in a number of other ways within the law to change it. But, he does not defy the law.

It is true that some dissenters commit violence, but they are comparatively few and their activities should not characterize all who are in dissent. Each of us, whether articulately or not is from time to time in dissent from something or other in our society and government. If we were not, there could be no progress. Everything would become static, and deterioration would set in. It is almost a rule of thumb that progress stems from dissent. "Dissent," then, should be an honored word, and all citizens should be encouraged to engage in it. The opposite of dissent is conformity, and nothing could be more deadly than to have conformity for the sake of conformity.

There is a vast difference, however, between dissent and defiance, although many fail to make the distinction. Some consider all dissent to be defiance, while counterminded extremists believe that the right to dissent includes the right to defy. Still others, advocating violence to seek ends they consider justifiable, defend their destructive conduct by equating it with the principle of the nineteenth-century philosopher and naturalist Henry Thoreau, who, in his essay "Civil Disobedience," justified passive resistance to laws that the citizen considers an invasion of his rights. Thoreau's personal disobedience consisted only of withdrawing from society, living alone on an isolated New England pond, and refusing to pay a tax. For this latter offense he submitted himself to arrest and imprisonment. His gentle philosophy was followed in our time by that of Gandhi and the late Dr. Martin Luther King.

A dictionary definition of civil disobedience, derived largely from the essay by Thoreau, reads:

*The refusal to obey certain governmental laws or demands for the purpose of influencing legislation or governmental policy characterized by the employment of such non-violent techniques as boycotting, picketing and non-payment of taxes.*

Civil disobedience neither advocates nor justifies violent conduct of any kind. It follows that it is a distortion of the spirit and intent of "civil disobedience" to quote the term as the authority for excusing crime, violence, subversive activities or underground activities of any kind.

In assessing "dissent" and "defiance," it is fair

to say that dissent is therapeutic. It is one of the most potent forces available to us for curing evils and righting wrongs. Forceful defiance or secret evasion of law, on the other hand, cures nothing. It is provocative of counterviolence and ultimate repression and, where it succeeds, leaves anarchy in its wake. Dissent advances the democratic process; defiance destroys it.

Included in the right to dissent is the right to appeal to the courts for the annulment of laws considered violative of the Constitution or for relief from what might be considered oppressive action by governmental officers or private persons. While such an appeal is often expensive as well as cumbersome, there is a growing sense of responsibility on the part of the legal profession in recent years to protect the rights of minority groups and of poor people who are unable to bear the cost of litigation.*

---

* In most of the larger communities and in many of the small, inquiry will disclose a legal organization committed to the protection of human rights for those who do not have the financial means to protect themselves. Some are publicly supported agencies; others are legal aid societies supported by Community Chests or bar associations, and often there are available public-spirited lawyers who will undertake such cases gratuitously. Many through the years have suffered wrongs and indignities rather than invoke the jurisdiction of our courts, not only because of the financial strain or the time consumed, but because they are unaware of the real purpose of the courts in our governmental system. They have viewed the courts as agencies to which only people of means subject their differences for adjustment. But this concept is being dissipated day by day as more and more of the poor discover their rights can be, and are, protected by courts against the most powerful elements in the community.

106

Still, the world is in a divisive and petulant mood. It has been in a warlike stance—hot, cold, lukewarm—for so long that tempers are frayed and fears fed by frustration. Ugly rhetoric too often has supplanted reason, and distrust is rampant. As a result, time-honored institutions are being discredited, and gaps have sprung up between nations, races, generations, the sexes, and the affluent and the poor.

In the solution of our problems, we must work on the incidental problem of closer communication through popular discussion. We have discovered how to do this in considering many issues. For instance, it took decades to establish means of communication between capital and labor, but, once we discovered how to do it, collective bargaining became the rule in almost every business and industry in the nation.

Formerly, intense hatred was generated between employer and employee in many industries. Many controversies were concluded only after massive strikes, marked by violence on both sides, that left everyone the loser, including the public. They left great scars, and threatened the survival of our economic system. Most of the violence has now disappeared. Differences between employer and employee over wages and working conditions still exist, and will probably continue to do so throughout the foreseeable future. But these disagreements are no longer considered a menace to the nation. On the contrary, they are looked upon as a phenomenon of our economic system, subject to solution through the bargaining process between the respective parties as equals, and often with the assistance of a mediator representative of the public interest.

Although we can never have a perfect society, we can have a wholesome one that will accommodate the needs of all without regard to race, color, creed, or social or economic status. The Scriptures wisely admonish us to reason and counsel together for:

*Where no counsel is, the people fall; but in the multitude of counsellors there is safety.*

Human nature has not changed, nor will it. Many institutions and governments designed for the well-being of mankind have been wiped out through neglect, and a number of experiments in democratic civilization have been buried beyond recall. If we are to overcome the divisiveness that pervades the world today, we need to be guided in our actions by reason rather than prejudice, and by the American manners of another day which manifested the good will that can flow from a sense of equality and from the recognition of human dignity in all persons.

# X

# THE BILL OF RIGHTS—I

*We hold these Truths to be Self evident, that all men are created equal, that they are endowed by their Creator with certain unalienable rights, that among these are Life, Liberty and the Pursuit of Happiness.*

THE FOUNDATION for "Life, Liberty and the Pursuit of Happiness" resides in the Bill of Rights. Were it not for the freedoms of speech, of the press, of religion, of association, of the right to petition the government, of the right of the accused to a public jury trial, to counsel and to be confronted by any witnesses against him, as well as freedom from unreasonable searches and seizures, our Constitution could, indeed, be a sterile document. None of these provisions, of course, was completely original with the Founding Fathers. Each of them was inspired by accumulated knowledge of persecution and human suffering, not only in the colonies and in England, but throughout recorded history wherever one man or a group of men unrestrained have been empowered to control the lives of the people.

In 1970 the Columbia Broadcasting System conducted a broadly based national poll to determine public reaction to the Bill of Rights—with disturbing results. Three fourths of those questioned would restrict the right of peaceful assembly; a majority would abridge the right of free speech and of the press, and the right of a person to be informed of the criminal charges against him, as well as to confront the witnesses against him at his trial. A third of those questioned would permit the police to search a person's house without a search warrant, and a fifth of them were even opposed to the right to a public trial.

In my own State of California, I am embarrassed to report, there occurred an incident, given only minor attention in the press, which was of shocking import. In 1955 President Eisenhower, in accordance with custom, declared September 16th, the date of the enactment of the Bill of Rights, to be National Bill of Rights Day. At one of the major buildings of the state, which was under the management of a retired army general, there was a bulletin board open to use by officials and state employees for public announcement of interest to either. The employees, following the President's proclamation, posted a copy of the Bill of Rights on the board. It was immediately taken down by the general with the statement that it was a controversial document and not fit for exposure on the board. The employees, protesting, put another copy in its place. It in turn was taken down by the superintendent for the same reason. The employees then took the case to the governor, and not until he had certified in writing that the document was appropriate for display on the bulletin board was it permitted to remain there.

This experience, of course, was a product of the days of Senator Joseph McCarthy when the country became so emotionalized by the fear of Communism that any liberal or humanitarian thought was likely to be considered subversive. Even a large segment of college students believed that the provisions of the Bill of Rights were outdated, and not essential to our way of life. Today —largely because of the fear of crime in the streets, student demonstrations and racial conflict—the older generation is seriously questioning the wisdom of retaining a number of the provisions of the Bill of Rights.

It is difficult to believe that those who would give up these basic rights really have considered or understood the full import of what they are saying, or that they are aware of how and why those protections found their way into the Constitution. Undoubtedly, more rights are eventually lost through neglect or ignorance than from outright abrogation. And this will continue to be true unless we relate the experience which brought our freedoms into existence to the ever-changing facts of life.

Of the Bill of Rights, Thomas Jefferson said: "A Bill of Rights is what the people are entitled to against any government on earth, general or particular, and what no just government should refuse or rest on inference." The provisions of our Bill of Rights are interrelated and can be roughly grouped into three classifications: (1) freedom of religion; (2) freedom of speech, the press and assembly or, more generally speaking, the rights of expression and association; and (3) freedom from arbitrary restraint or trial and from cruel and unusual punishment. This interrelationship was dramatized in the notorious case against William Penn, the founder of Pennsylvania, shortly before his coming to America.

Penn was a leader of the Quakers in London. The sect was not recognized by the government and was forbidden to meet in any building for the purpose of worship. In 1670 William Penn held a worship service in a quiet street which was attended by a peaceful group of fellow Quakers. Penn and another Quaker, William Mead, were arrested on a charge of disturbing the King's peace and summoned to stand trial. As the two men entered the courtroom, a bailiff ordered them to place their hats, which they had removed, back on their heads. When they complied, they were called forward and held in contempt of court for being in the courtroom with their hats on.

That was only the beginning. Penn demanded to know under which law they were charged. The court refused to supply that information and instead referred vaguely to the common law. When Penn protested that he was entitled to a specific indictment, he was removed from the presence of the judge and jury and confined in an enclosed corner of the room known as the baledock. From there, he could neither confront the witnesses who accused him of preaching to the Quakers nor ask them questions about their charges against him.

Several witnesses testified that Penn had preached to a gathering which included Mead, but one showed some hesitancy as to whether Mead had been present. The judge turned to Mead and questioned him directly. In essence, he was asking Mead if he were guilty. Mead invoked the common-law privilege against self-incrimination which provoked hostile comment from the judge. The court then sent Mead to join Penn in the bale-dock out of the sight of the jury and witnesses. After the testimony the court instructed the jury to find the defendants guilty as charged. Penn tried to protest, but was silenced and again sent out of the courtroom.

The jury, for its part, proved sympathetic to the two defendants, and refused the judge's command to find the defendants guilty. The judge was furious and sent them away to reconsider. When they returned with the same verdict, the court criticized the jury's leader, one Bushnell, and demanded "a verdict that the court will accept, and you shall be locked up without meat, drink, fire, and tobacco. . . . We will have a verdict by the help of God or you will starve for it."

Three more times the jury went out and returned with the same verdict. Finally, they refused to go out any more. The judge fined each of them forty marks and ordered them imprisoned until the fine was paid. Penn and Mead went to prison anyway for obeying the bailiff's order that they put on their hats. Later a writ of habeas corpus won freedom for the jurors while Penn and Mead left jail to come to America.

Penn's own account of the case was printed in pamphlet form and widely distributed throughout the colonies. Most Americans interested in law and politics had read it and understood its significance. During the debate in Congress on the first Ten Amendments, soon to become the Bill of Rights, Penn's case was mentioned in support of the need for specific guarantees of individual liberty to worship, to speak, to associate peacefully with others, to be free from arbitrary and unjust courtroom procedures and to have impartial juries.

The case of William Penn alone indicates clearly that the colonists were not dealing in abstractions but in actual experiences. And their determination to right the other evils inflicted under British law is evident throughout the Constitution and its first amendments.

The first, and perhaps the most important, amendment of the Bill of Rights reads:

AMENDMENT I

*Congress shall make no law respecting an establishment of religion or prohibiting the free exercise thereof; or abridging the freedom of speech, or of the press; or the right of the people peaceably to assemble and to petition the Government for a redress of grievances.*

Significantly prime consideration was given to freedom of religion because the history of both England and the colonies proved that without the freedom to believe and to practice one's own faith other freedoms shrink into insignificance.

"In the 16th century," wrote one historian, "the history of the church is the history of England. Catholics and Protestants alike recognized the duty of the state to uphold truth and repress error. . . . Conformity with the new faith, as with the old, was enforced by the dungeon, the scaffold, the gibbet and the torch."

The case of William Penn was thus only a more recent illustration of religious fanaticism. Much of the tyranny which the framers of the Constitution feared stemmed from religious intolerance. The history of Europe gave too many examples of wars fought, men and groups persecuted, and suffering wrought because of religious opinion which diverged from that held by those who wielded the most power.

A half-century after the adoption of the First Amendment, a disgraceful chapter of our own history was enacted in Philadelphia, the so-called City of Brotherly Love founded by William Penn as a consequence of the religious persecution he suffered in England. The trouble arose out of a school controversy over the requirement that prayer and Bible reading be solely from the Protestant Bible. In late 1842, the Catholic Bishop of Philadelphia requested the school officials to permit Catholic children to read their own version of the Bible. The Board of Comptrollers of the Public Schools agreed with the Bishop and permitted the children to read any version of the Bible their parents selected. This action aroused the ire of the American Protestant Association, a militant, anti-Catholic organization. Because of its propaganda, feelings of hatred and intolerance for Catholics increased amongst the Protestant congregations.

The result was prolonged rioting in 1844. Catholics feared for their lives. Churches were burned. Priests and nuns went underground. People on both sides were killed, and much property, mostly homes of Irish Catholic families, was destroyed. These riots shame the memory of those founders of the nation who believed that religion is and ought to be each person's private affair. The First Amendment underwrites the admonition of Thomas Jefferson that there should be a wall of separation between church and state.*

---

* In 1787, in some of the original states, public officials—Senators, Congressmen and legislators included—were required to be of the Protestant faith. A provision of this kind in the Constitution of the State of New Hampshire was not repealed until 1852, and a similar requirement for schoolteachers was retained to a later date. Also, until

There have been sporadic outbursts of religious intolerance since that date. As late in our history as 1925, the State of Tennessee enacted a law prohibiting the teaching in public schools of theories contrary to accepted interpretation of the Biblical account of man's creation. A young science teacher, John T. Scopes, was prosecuted in the same year for teaching the evolutionary theories of Charles Darwin in a public school. The trial commanded world-wide attention because of the prominent counsels in the case, William Jennings Bryan for the prosecution and Clarence Darrow for the defendant. Scopes was convicted, but the Supreme Court of Tennessee reversed the decision on other than First Amendment ground, thus freeing Scopes but leaving the statute in force. Arkansas had a similar statute prohibiting such teaching in its schools or universities. In 1967 the Supreme Court of that State sustained the statute. The Supreme Court of the United States, in reversing the decision, said:

*There is and can be no doubt that the First Amendment does not permit the State to require that teaching and learning must be tailored to the*

---

1960, there was a prevailing opinion in the country that a Catholic, regardless of his qualifications, could not be elected President of the United States. Happily that specter of intolerance was laid to rest by the election of President John Fitzgerald Kennedy, a Catholic.

*principles or prohibitions of any religious sect or dogma.*

Few such opportunities in this field have ever reached the Supreme Court. But in recent years another case, this time from Pennsylvania, came to that court as a result of state procedures prescribing officially prepared and required prayers and Bible reading for the children of the public schools, without regard to the religion of parents or pupils. A number of religious groups appealed to the Court to nullify the procedures as being an abridgment of the religious rights of their children and, therefore, an infringement by the government.

The Court, in recognition of past experiences, had this to say in striking down the requirements:

*Freedom to worship was indispensable in a country whose people came from the four corners of the earth and brought with them a diversity of religious opinion. Today authorities list 83 separate religious bodies, each with membership exceeding 50,000, existing among our people as well as innumerable smaller groups. . . . The place of religion in our society is an exalted one, achieved through a long tradition of reliance on the home, the church, and the inviolable citadel of the individual heart and mind. We have come to realize through bitter experience that it is not within the power of government to invade that citadel, whether its purpose or effect be to aid or oppose, to advance or retard. In the relationship between man and religion, the state is firmly committed to a position of neutrality.*

Freedom of speech, of the press, of assembly, and to petition the government are also protected by the First Amendment. These are related to freedom of religion because the right to believe is circumscribed almost beyond usefulness unless one is allowed to express himself orally or in writing to listeners or to readers, or to assemble with others for the purpose of expressing his religious faith or his political views

These rights have been fairly well preserved to date largely because of the universal determination by the press of America to protect the freedom of speech and other forms of expression.

And it is well that the press maintains such a stance because the public has the right to be informed of the actions of those who carry on the affairs of government as their representatives. There has long been a tendency, as government has grown, to withhold information that the public should have for its guidance in voting and petitioning its elected representatives and other officials. Only recently two metropolitan newspapers whose daily concern is national affairs, *The New York Times* and *The Washington Post,* published some of the contents of the "History of United States Decision-making Process on Vietnam Policy," prepared for the then Secretary of Defense, Robert McNamara, by a special task force in the Pentagon. Although this report had been distributed within the government in a limited way some years ago, it has remained classified "Top Secret" and its contents denied to the public. The act under which it was so classified prohibited the divulgence of such classified material by those who had custody of it, but did not prohibit its publication in the event it was divulged.

The government sought an injunction in the federal courts to restrain publication on the ground that the President, under his prerogatives as Commander-in-Chief and in the conduct of foreign affairs, has inherent powers which entitle him to an injunction to prevent the publication as news of anything that, in his opinion, would bring irreparable injury to the public interest. Such an injunction would constitute what is known in the law as prior restraint.

On June 30, 1971, the Supreme Court held that neither the President nor the courts have any such powers under the First Amendment, and the injunction was denied.

The rule against prior restraint has a long and honorable history in both English and American law. It was set forth emphatically in the English

Commentaries of William Blackstone whose works were so popular in America at the time of the adoption of our Constitution. It was designed to protect the freedom of the press to expose for the benefit of the people the frailties, the malfeasance and the corruption of public officials.

Although previous to the cases mentioned above no attempt had been made by the Federal Government to enforce prior restraint, Chief Justice Hughes forty years ago in the case of *Near* v. *Minnesota* said:

> . . . *the administration of government has become more complex, the opportunities for malfeasance and corruption have multipled, crime has grown to most serious proportions, and the danger of its protection by unfaithful officials and of the impairment of the fundamental security of life and property by criminal alliances and official neglect, emphasizes the primary need of a vigilant and courageous press, especially in great cities. The fact that the liberty of the press may be abused by miscreant purveyors of scandal does not make any the less necessary the immunity of the press from previous restraint in dealing with official misconduct.*

And in a later case, *de Jonge* v. *Oregon*, Chief Justice Hughes wrote:

122

*The greater the importance of safeguarding the community from incitements to the overthrow of our institutions by force and violence, the more imperative is the need to preserve inviolate the constitutional rights of free speech, free press and free assembly in order to maintain the opportunity for free political discussion, to the end that government may be responsive to the will of the people and that changes, if desired, may be obtained by peaceful means. Therein lies the security of the Republic, the very foundation of constitutional government.*

The rights of assembly and to petition the government or dissent from it are part and parcel of the right of freedom of speech and usually come under the umbrella of its protection. Still memory is often very short. It was only a few years after the First Amendment was established that the infamous Alien and Sedition Laws were passed by the Congress primarily to suppress the newly formed Republican Party of Thomas Jefferson.

Many of the new arrivals from Europe became adherents of that party, and Jefferson's opponents, who controlled the government, put severe restrictions on the immigrants, lengthened the period of residence required for their naturalization from five to fourteen years and gave the President power to expel them from the country if, in his opinion, they were subversive.

These laws treated as seditious and, therefore, criminal almost all criticism of the government. As a practical matter, they nullified the express provisions of the First Amendment. Prominent citizens were tried and convicted under them until the election of Jefferson in 1800, when they were repealed. Ever since they have been subjects of scorn.

Notwithstanding this object lesson, there have been occasional attempts in times of public hysteria to abridge these precious First Amendment rights. In the days of the late Senator Joseph McCarthy the rights of speech and association were put in serious jeopardy through "loyalty oaths," legislative investigations solely for the sake of exposure and irresponsible speeches in Congress charging citizens with subversion or of associating with alleged subversives. Fortunately, many of the so-called loyalty oaths were invalidated, the effects of legislative exposure for the sake of exposure were circumscribed either by the courts or by change of Congressional rules, and vitriolic speeches were subdued by the temper of Congress itself in response to public opinion. But the danger of repression is always present wherever and whenever men possess great power. We must guard against it constantly if we are to preserve the freedoms it would destroy.

The Second Amendment, which is attracting some attention at present, has not often been brought under judicial review.

AMENDMENT II

*A well regulated Militia being necessary to the security of a free state, the right of the people to keep and bear arms shall not be infringed.*

Under Amendment II, most of the states and the federal government have dealt in various but ineffectual ways with the illegal possession of guns. The need for more effective laws has mounted in recent years because of the increase in violent crimes, most of which involve the use of guns. Confronted with this appalling situation, many members of Congress have introduced or supported bills for adequate gun control. But to date the so-called "gun lobby" has managed to defeat them and the problem continues to accelerate day by day.

For 1969 the FBI reported 14,587 murders, 36,470 forcible rapes, 297,584 robberies, 306,420 aggravated assaults, and 1,949,843 burglaries. The vast majority of the murders and robberies, and a large percentage of the other crimes, were committed with handguns. Yet many people oppose gun control, contending it would be in violation of the Second Amendment. This is not the fact.

The courts have pointed out that the Second Amendment links the "right to keep and bear arms" with a "well regulated Militia." At the time of the writing of the Constitution, the states constituted, for the most part, a frontier society on the edge of the unknown. Some of the states required every male to have a gun, a certain amount of ammunition and equipment for service in the militia in times of community danger. It was with honor and pride that young men equipped themselves for such service. The Founding Fathers had implicit faith in a militia because their experiences with the British had made standing armies abhorrent to them. As a consequence, through the Second Amendment, they guaranteed the right of the states to maintain the militia and accorded the people the right to bear arms for that purpose. Additionally, society tacitly acknowledged that, in wild frontier country, guns were needed in hunting for food and protection against marauders, whether man or beast. Such weapons were almost always long guns. The handgun played relatively little part in frontier action. Today the handgun is a menace beyond description. Because of changes in community responsibilities as we developed from a pioneer society to a rural and urban society, the same concern for the security of the community which prompted the use of rifles and shotguns in earlier days should now cause people to regulate the use and possession of guns which can be used with such terrible effect in the commission of so many crimes.

The Third Amendment was born of the feeling against the practice of the British forcibly quartering their troops in the homes of the colonists during the later colonial days. It reads as follows:

AMENDMENT III

*No soldier shall in time of peace be quartered in any house without the consent of the owner nor in time of war but in a manner to be prescribed by law.*

This amendment has not been tested in the courts and so far as is known has never been violated.

The development of the Fourth Amendment, which had been in process for centuries under Anglo-Saxon law, was accelerated when colonial courts appointed by the Crown issued general warrants to their officers to enter and search any house or individual for contraband thought to have been smuggled into the colonies without payment of duty. No reason was required for the search or the probability of finding contraband on the person or the property, and, as could be expected from such unlimited power, the privacy of citizens was repeatedly invaded and injuries inflicted on innocent persons. The colonists bitterly resented these invasions as contrary to the English principle that every man's home is his castle as stated by the elder William Pitt shortly before the American Revolution: "The poorest man may in his cottage bid defiance to all the force of the Crown. It may be frail; its roof may leak; the wind may blow through it; the storm may enter, but the King of England cannot enter. All his force dares not cross the threshold of the ruined tenement."

The colonists cherished this concept of the privacy of home and person. They rejected the theory that only people who have something to hide mind having their homes searched or being stopped, searched and questioned by the police. They accordingly provided:

### AMENDMENT IV

*The right of the people to be secure in their persons, houses, papers, and effects, against unreasonable searches and seizures, shall not be violated, and no Warrants shall issue, but upon probable cause, supported by Oaths or affirmation, and particularly describing the place to be searched, and the persons or things to be seized.*

The Fourth Amendment strikes a balance between the right of privacy and the need to have evidence of a crime by requiring, as a preliminary to a search, a warrant based upon a reasonably specific justification, under oath, for the particular search and "particularly describing the place to be searched and the persons or things to be seized." When the letter and spirit of this amendment are properly observed, the needs of the public in law enforcement are protected without disturbing the right of privacy. This has been eloquently expressed by Mr. Justice Brandeis:

*The makers of our Constitution undertook to secure conditions favorable to the pursuit of happiness. They recognized the significance of man's spiritual nature, of his feelings and of his intellect. They knew that only a part of the pain, pleasure and satisfaction of life are to be found in material things. They sought to protect Americans in their beliefs, their thoughts, their emotions and their sensations. They conferred, as against the government, the right to be let alone—the most comprehensive of rights and the right most valued by civilized men. To protect that right, every unjustifiable intrusion by the government upon the privacy of the individual, whatever the means employed, must be deemed a violation of the Fourth Amendment. And the use, as evidence, in a criminal proceeding of facts ascertained by such intrusion must be deemed a violation of the Fifth.*

Vital as this concept of privacy was in 1789, or even as it was forty years ago when it was championed by Mr. Justice Brandeis, it is far more vital and important in the lives of Americans today.

When the Fourth Amendment was adopted, an illegal invasion of a private home or place of business could only be made against the will of the owner by force or, in his absence, by stealth. Today not only can telephone wires be tapped but, by more sophisticated electronic equipment, the privacy of a home and all of its activities can be violated with little or no chance of the invader being detected.

Thus the Fourth Amendment is being violated by some authorities indiscriminately, and in several of our largest cities the use of legal search warrants is becoming almost a lost art. This is a condition fraught with great danger to the freedom of Americans, and should be scrutinized with care to make certain that the prohibition against unreasonable searches is not further eroded. If any one person's rights can be violated with impunity, then everyone's can be.

# XI

## THE BILL OF RIGHTS—II

IT IS both distressing and short-sighted for so many people to be of the opinion that matters of procedure are simply escape hatches for criminals, or "mere technicalities." The truth is that questions which we call procedural are prime essentials in an orderly society. To demean their importance is to say that respect and tolerance for others is not a requisite for freedom and liberty.

Procedural safeguards, such as the right to cross-examine witnesses or the privilege against self-incrimination, are what distinguish our judicial system from the proverbial kangaroo court. So it is hoped that whatever falls within the compass of these safeguards will be recognized as something too important to be left only to lawyers; assuring that these procedures are followed is the responsibility of every one of us.

The Fifth and Sixth Amendments established twelve requirements for the actual trial of criminal cases. These requirements are interrelated and should be read together:

### AMENDMENT V

*No person shall be held to answer for a capital, or otherwise infamous crime, unless on a presentment or indictment of a Grand Jury, except in cases arising in the land or naval forces, or in the Militia, when in actual service in time of War or public danger; nor shall any person be subject for the same offence to be twice put in jeopardy of life or limb; nor shall be compelled in any criminal case to be a witness against himself; nor be deprived of life, liberty, or property, without due process of law; nor shall private property be taken for public use without just compensation.*

### AMENDMENT VI

*In all criminal prosecutions, the accused shall enjoy the right to a speedy and public trial, by an impartial jury of the State and district wherein the crime shall have been committed, which district shall have been previously ascer-*

*tained by law, and to be informed of the nature and cause of the accusation; to be confronted with the witnesses against him; to have compulsory process for obtaining witnesses in his favor, and to have the Assistance of Counsel for his defence.*

Most of these safeguards were intended to prevent the excesses perpetrated under the English Court of the Star Chamber which was finally abolished in 1641. This court symbolized to the colonists, as well as free men everywhere, the worst form of a system of criminal justice. Its purpose was to provide a swift and efficient way to strike down the robber bands which were terrorizing the English countryside and to punish the castle owners who provided them sanctuary for a share in the loot. The Star Chamber was effective precisely because it allowed the King and his Council to bypass all of the procedural safeguards which had grown up under common law.

For speed and certainty, the Chamber brought people to trial by "information ex officio" —that is, by having them arrested on the order of the Chamber and nothing more. No grand jury indictment and no probable cause for arrest stood in the way of bringing a person to trial. This procedure was coupled with the "oath ex officio" which men suspected of crime were compelled to take. This oath required these men to answer all ques-

133

tions as to their guilt or innocence. There was no privilege against self-incrimination; no right to remain silent and have the government prove its case. The judges were the triers of fact. No jury stood between their desires, and the defendant. Punishment which the Chamber inflicted included imprisonment up to life, fines, pillory, whipping, branding and mutilation.

Irving Brant* has described the progress of the Star Chamber as an instrument of oppression:

*The Star Chamber did, indeed, prove efficient, and for many years its popularity was high. . . . But like all possessors of arbitrary power, it was corrupted by its own authority and its methods. Turning from the chastisement of robbers to the suspension of political and religious freedoms, it made injustice swift, sure and terrible. Men who made the slightest deviation from orthodoxy as to King or church were liable to be dragged off to London and put on trial by the fiat of the prosecutor. Defendants were forced to answer incriminating questions. Confessions were obtained by torture. Punishment was as certain as death and lacking little of its terrors. The primary procedures*

---

* The narrow compass of this book will not accommodate a treatment of many of the cases which influenced early Americans, but Irving Brant's book, *The Bill of Rights—Its Origin and Meaning*, details the specific incidents of injustice which aroused the colonists. It is worth reading by any American citizen.

*—torture, etc.—spread to the common law courts. King's Bench jurors who found political defendants not guilty were dragged to the Star Chamber for punishment.*

Few courts or tribunals can match the Star Chamber as an instrument of injustice and oppression; it remains today as a reminder that unfettered power to administer the criminal sanction, and single-minded determination to punish criminals, without a corresponding concern for the rights of every individual, will undermine a free society.

The indictment—provided for in the first clause of the Fifth Amendment—is essential to our system because it specifies the crime for which a person is being prosecuted, and establishes probable cause to believe he committed it. It is the premise upon which the second clause, referring to double jeopardy, is predicated. The specificity of charge in the indictment enables a person to establish his right under this clause if he has once been tried and acquitted or convicted of any public offense. The protection is of great importance to everyone. Without it a person once charged with a crime would never be out of the power of the authorities because if he should be acquitted, or even convicted and imprisoned, he could again be tried and convicted of the identical offense.

The third clause of the Fifth Amendment is

one of the most controversial and sometimes the least understood provision of the Bill of Rights—"nor shall be compelled in any criminal case to be a witness against himself."

The case of John Lilburne is often cited as the first use of the privilege in its full modern meaning. In 1637 the Star Chamber ordered Lilburne to take an oath by which he would swear to answer all questions which might be asked of him. In his famous reply, he asserted his privilege against self-incrimination: "I know it is warrantable by the law of God and I think by the law of the land that I may stand upon my just defense and not answer to your interrogatories, and that my accusers ought to be brought face to face to justify what they accuse me of." For this answer, he was whipped and imprisoned indefinitely. Three years later in 1640, he was vindicated in his statement of the law when Parliament ordered his release from prison, and the House of Lords commenced an inquiry into the legality of Lilburne's trial and imprisonment. The Lords concluded that Lilburne had been correct in insisting on his privilege to have the case against him proved by other than his own statements.

Today the privilege of not testifying on matters which might be self-incriminating applies not only to a person in police custody accused of a crime, or when he is on trial, but also to those who are called as witnesses at a trial or before a grand jury or investigating committee. It is a right honored throughout the Anglo-Saxon world but many people fail to understand its significance, particularly those who have never been faced with an accusation. They reason that if a person is not guilty he need have nothing to hide by refusing to be questioned. But life is not that simple. Many times, because of what appears to be damning circumstances, the finger of suspicion points to a person innocent of any wrongdoing.

Not all persons under suspicion are guilty of an offense. Under our system, a person cannot be arrested for a crime unless, in the opinion of the responsible authorities, there is probable cause to believe he is guilty of the offense. Statistics reported to the FBI by 3,999 police departments show that in 1969 over three million arrests were made for major crimes, yet only a small fraction of those arrested were tried, or were convicted after pleading guilty. What became of the others? They were released for lack of evidence. However, if all of them could have been *compelled* to testify against themselves, undoubtedly many more would have been convicted—and among them many innocent persons found guilty because of circumstances they could not explain.

For murder and all other capital crimes, there is no statute of limitations—no period after which immunity from prosecution obtains—and a person may be prosecuted any number of years after a crime has been committed. In the federal system, all other crimes have a five-year statute of limitations. In the states, the period varies. But in either federal or state jurisdictions, many persons are prosecuted years after a crime has taken place. If they could be compelled at such times to try to explain away suspicious circumstances which occurred long in the past they would be subjected to unwarranted peril. It is for this reason that the prosecution is required to establish, through facts, guilt beyond and to the exclusion of all reasonable doubt to justify conviction. That is one of the great safeguards of our system of justice.

Any departure from this requirement, such as obtaining confessions by force (the notorious "third degree") would be oppressive and, therefore, contrary to the intention of the Founding Fathers. There are countries where such use of physical and mental torture to obtain confessions is the order of the day. Accusing a person of the commission of a crime is an awesome yet essential power under our system of jurisprudence, but the power to compel a man to convict himself by his own testimony is an instrument of torture and injustice. A wrong word, the honest admission of some compromising fact, or even understandable nervousness and fear might be enough to make an innocent person's protestations lack credibility.

The Fifth Amendment also provides in criminal cases that no person shall "be deprived of life, liberty, or property, without due process of law." The phrase "due process of law" is a compendious one, encompassing all the basic protections guaranteed by the Constitution. It is of ancient origin and can be traced directly to an English law enacted in 1355 which provided that "No man, of what state or condition he be, shall be put out of his land or tenements nor be put to death without he be brought to answer by due process of law." This statute, in turn, was based on the Magna Carta of 1214, and is still honored in England as it is in our country.

The final clause of the amendment protects the right of the people to be secure in their property against government seizure through confiscation, conscription or other device. We often read of "expropriation" taking place in other countries—in other words, the taking of property without compensation or without the recognition of any private rights. The right to possess property lawfully acquired is a right which cannot be dissociated from human rights.

One of the most significant rights a citizen can have is his right to be tried by jury. The first clause of the Sixth Amendment protects that right and it has two essential aspects: the jury must be impartial—not subject to any prejudice or outside influence; and the jurors must be chosen from the local area in which the crime was committed to serve in the trial held in that same area. These guarantees were especially valued by the men who fought the American Revolution and who insisted on a bill of rights in their Constitution. The colonists found more and more of their litigation decided by judges sitting without a jury in admiralty or administrative courts; furthermore, a person suspected of committing any act of treason (that term covered a vast number of situations) could be taken to England for trial even if the act of which he was accused happened in the colonies.*

The right to a jury trial is now well accepted, but the disputes about the full enjoyment of that right have arisen throughout our history. As long ago as 1880, the Supreme Court said that a Negro did not have an impartial jury if his race was sys-

---

* Concern for the future of the traditional jury reached a peak after a band of Rhode Island men, angered by the harassment of traffic in Narragansett Bay by British Men of War attacked His Majesty's schooner "Gaspee," and burned the ship to ashes. An announcement warned that the act was treason, and it was widely believed that the perpetrators, when caught, would be sent to England to stand trial.

*The Providence Gazette* summarized the lesson the colonists had learned on the eve of the American Revolution:

*In this situation of affairs, every friend of our violated Constitution cannot but be greatly alarmed. The idea of seizing a number of persons under the point of bayonets and transporting them three thousand miles for trial where, whether guilty or innocent, they must unavoidably fall victims alike to revenge or prejudice. It is shocking to humanity, repugnant to every detail of reason, liberty and justice, and in which Americans and free men ought never to acquiesce.*

tematically excluded from the list from which jury members were selected. Since then our courts have been obliged to decide many similar cases in like manner. The basic principle has remained the same —an impartial jury is one which is drawn from a broad section of the community.

Another source of dispute has been the inter-action of civilian and military courts. In the military system, the trial is by court-martial; that is, a number of officers selected by the commanding officer who judge the facts and the law of the case. The Supreme Court has made clear that this exception to the right of civilian jury is very narrow. Two cases decided in 1955 provide good examples. In the first, a man named Toth was honorably discharged from the Air Force after having served in Korea. He went home to Pittsburgh, obtained a job in a steel plant, and worked there for five months before he was arrested by military police, hurriedly flown back to Korea, and charged with the murder of another Air Force man while both were in the service. The Supreme Court, on habeas corpus, released him from detention for trial by a court-martial, pointing out that as soon as Toth was released from the service he was a civilian and as such entitled to a jury trial in a civil court. Had the decision been otherwise, any of the millions of servicemen, after being honorably discharged, could be dragged back to a distant part of the world and be tried there by court-martial without any of the protections of a jury trial.

In the second case, two women were charged with killing their servicemen husbands while the families were stationed abroad. The women and the cases were unrelated, but raised the same issue. In both cases the defense was insanity, which is an issue to be decided by a jury according to the legal standards in civilian courts. But these women were tried by courts-martial according to a law passed by Congress which provided that military courts had jurisdiction over dependents of servicemen stationed abroad. The Supreme Court decided that the Bill of Rights forbade such a trial, at least in time of peace, and held that the women were entitled to a jury trial in civilian courts. Had it not been for this decision, the wives, children and parents of servicemen who went overseas with them could be tried by a military court thousands of miles away from home, friends, witnesses, and the opportunity to defend themselves adequately, or even be returned to such distant places for that purpose after they had come home.

These cases show that a citizen's right to a jury trial can still be preserved only through vigilance, and, once more, it is our responsibility to keep it that way.

But the right to a jury trial would not mean very much if the accused person were denied the right to present his defense in an effective manner. Simply having twelve honest and impartial jurors is not enough to protect liberty. The Sixth Amendment contains, in addition to its guarantee of a jury from the local area, six provisions which ensure that the accused will be able to tell his side of the story effectively. The trial must be speedy and public—speedy so that the witnesses for and against the accused will remain available and so that their memories will be relatively fresh; open so that public opinion and scrutiny can act as forces for compliance with fair procedures and as checks to short cuts in the taking of evidence or other abuse of power which disadvantage the defendant.

Next, the defendant must be informed of the nature and cause of the accusation. This clause is a restatement of the common-law rule requiring that the charge in the indictment against the defendant be set out with enough precision and detail to enable him to prepare his defense and to afford him the protection of the double jeopardy clause should he be subsequently prosecuted for the same crime.

Two other rights guaranteed by the Sixth Amendment deal with the witnesses who give their version of facts to the jury. "In all criminal prosecutions, the accused shall enjoy the right . . . to be confronted with the witnesses against him" and

143

"to have compulsory process for obtaining witnesses in his favor. . . ." These rights are essential
if the defendant is to have the opportunity to present his story to the jury. He must be able to confront the witnesses against him in order to question
them as to their sincerity, memory, perception and
bias. He must have compulsory process so that he
can command the presence in court of witnesses
who have information favorable to him.*

The last provision of the Sixth Amendment is
probably the most crucial—"The Assistance of
Counsel for his defence." Without a lawyer to help
him through the maze of legal procedures, a defendant might forfeit his other rights. This right has
a confusing history in common law, applying to
some crimes but not others. At the time of the
American Revolution, twelve of the thirteen states
recognized the importance of counsel in criminal

---

* One famous incident where these rights were denied made a deep
impression on early Americans. That was the trial of Sir Walter
Raleigh for treason. Raleigh was accused in 1603 of plotting to advance
Lady Arabella Stuart to the throne of England in order to bribe the
Archduke of Austria, the King of Spain, and the Duke of Savoy, and
thereby secure money and power for himself. The alleged plot was
complicated and in general terms seems far-fetched. The sole evidence
against Raleigh was the word of Lord Cobham who insisted that he was
Raleigh's co-conspirator in the plot and who was scheduled to stand
trial himself after Raleigh's trial was completed. Cobham's testimony
was taken by deposition, a procedure where the witness was questioned, his answers written down, and the writing introduced at the
trial. Raleigh's efforts to have Cobham produced in person so that he
could be proved a liar were futile. Raleigh was convicted and beheaded.
His trial was then and has since been considered a travesty of justice,
an example of a man's political enemies using the cover of judicial proceedings to assassinate him.

cases by providing for the right in their constitutions. Unfortunately, as so often happens with hard-won liberties, the right on paper does not assure the existence or the enjoyment of the right in practice. Not until 1938 was the rule established that poor defendants had a right to have a lawyer appointed to defend them in serious federal cases, and not until 1963 was this Constitutional right established in state courts.

One of the celebrated cases of the depression years was the Scottsboro case, *Powell* v. *Alabama.* Nine young Negroes were accused by two white girls of raping them during a freight train ride across Alabama in an open gondola car in which there were, in addition to the nine Negro defendants, seven white boys and two white girls. There had been a fight between the blacks and the whites, and all but one of the whites were ejected by the Negroes from the train. The defendants were arrested by a sheriff's posse because of the fight, and the rape accusation followed.

The nature of the crime and the color of the accused caused intense hostility toward them in Scottsboro where they were arrested. The militia was called out to prevent a lynching, and remained on duty throughout the brief time between arrest and trial, which was six days after indictment. At the time of the arraignment (the hearing in court where the charges are read to the prisoner, and he is asked to plead guilty or not guilty), the judge, learning that the defendants did not have a lawyer, with a wave of his hand appointed "all the members of the bar" to represent the defendants at the arraignment.

The nine men pleaded not guilty and were scheduled to be tried in four separate trials. At the trials, each of which lasted only one day, the same procedure for providing counsel was made, and no lawyer accepted the responsibility of representing them. All but one of the defendants were convicted of first-degree murder with a mandatory death sentence.

Each of the prisoners without a lawyer was, in the words of the Supreme Court, "young, ignorant, illiterate, surrounded by hostile sentiment, hailed back and forth under guard of soldiers," and because of these facts denied a fair trial. Representation by a lawyer would at least have ensured proper procedures at the trial.

Another example of the importance of counsel was the case of Tony Moreno, an eighteen-year-old boy who had been in this country for two years and was still unable to speak English at the time of his trial. He was charged with murder. He was alleged to have signed a written waiver of his right to a jury and to have pleaded guilty, but, as the state subsequently conceded, he did neither. He was at all times without the assistance of a lawyer, and was sentenced to life imprisonment one week after indictment. All his contacts with the judge who tried and sentenced him were through an interpreter who was the same officer who arrested him.

After he had spent twenty-two years in prison, the state admitted these facts, confessed error, and consented to his release on habeas corpus by the Supreme Court of the United States. The Court reversed his conviction, and vacated the sentence of life imprisonment because there was no showing that Tony Moreno even comprehended what was going on while he was in court.

Finally, in 1963, in the case of *Gideon* v. *Wainwright,* the Supreme Court decided that every person charged with a serious crime has a constitutional right to have a lawyer represent him, and in the event he cannot obtain one himself the state must procure one for him. The Scottsboro cases and that of Tony Moreno demonstrate how important it is for the poor, the illiterate and the underprivileged to have this protection. Everyone accused of crime needs such representation in order to have a fair trial. The affluent and the sophisticated know this, and are always able to obtain legal assistance themselves. The poor cannot, and without counsel they are helpless.

In recent years, these incidents have been reduced due to the present requirement that all persons, rich or poor, must now have a lawyer in serious criminal cases. There are those who criticize this expanded role for lawyers, insisting that the lawyer merely delays and hinders the search for truth in a trial by interposing technical objections. However, as long as we deal with criminal offenders in an adversary situation, each person must have the aid of a lawyer when he is accused of crime if our society is to continue to have faith in its judicial system. Otherwise, we cannot even be reasonably confident of punishing only the guilty. A society which does not insist on such confidence cannot expect its citizens to have confidence in the law.

The Seventh Amendment guarantees the right to a jury trial in civil cases.

### AMENDMENT VII

*In Suits at common law, where the value in controversy shall exceed twenty dollars, the right of trial by jury shall be preserved, and no fact tried by a jury, shall be otherwise reexamined in any Court of the United States, than according to the rules of the common law.*

The only other amendment in the Bill of Rights which pertains to procedures against persons accused of crime is the Eighth. It is an extremely important one, particularly for the poor.

AMENDMENT VIII

*Excessive bail shall not be required, nor excessive fines imposed, nor cruel and unusual punishment inflicted.*

The well-to-do defendant almost invariably can obtain bail and be released pending his trial, but the poor man must remain in jail, whether guilty or innocent, throughout the cumbersome court process unless understanding judges honor this amendment by requiring only so much bail as will ensure the defendant's presence at his trial.

In these days of congested court calendars, when trials are not accorded for many months, it is a gross injustice to compel poor persons accused of crimes to remain in jail while others charged with similar crimes are readily released on bail. Excessive fines are productive of similar injustice because the wealthy can always pay their fines, but the poor must serve jail terms because of their inability to do so.

And the prohibition against cruel and unusual punishment is not outmoded. There are nations which still inflict brutal punishments, and in every community there are some sadists against whom such a prohibition has a restraining influence.

The Ninth and Tenth Amendments simply make plain that in adopting the Bill of Rights the people were not excluding others that resided in them and that all powers not delegated to the federal government are reserved to the states or the people.

### AMENDMENT IX

*The enumeration in the Constitution of certain rights, shall not be construed to deny or disparage others retained by the people.*

### AMENDMENT X

*The powers not delegated to the United States by the Constitution, nor prohibited by it to the States, are reserved to the States respectively, or to the people.*

In addition to these ten amendments, there are four provisions of the Constitution itself so related to the Bill of Rights that they are often thought of as part of our charter of liberties. These are the prohibition on ex post facto laws, bills of attainder, religious tests for public office, and the guarantee of habeas corpus except in times of rebellion or invasion.

The ex post facto law is one which provides a punishment or penalty for some past act which, when it occurred, was not a crime. Fair-minded people have always recognized that ex post facto laws should not be allowed, but there are many examples of punishment imposed for behavior which was not a crime when it happened. In 1634, for example, William Prynne had the misfortune of being called before the Star Chamber because of a book he had written. His book condemned plays, dancing and other forms of public entertainment; one chapter was entitled, "Women Actors Notorious Whores." Unhappily the book was printed four years after he had finished writing it and only six weeks before the Queen of England made her dramatic debut in a stage play. His book, which would not have attracted much notice a few years earlier when it was written, became a crime. Prynne was fined 5,000 pounds, sentenced to stand successively at two pillories and have an ear cut off while confined in each, and spend the rest of his life in prison.

The trial of Prynne was over three centuries ago, but the temptation of people in times of great stress or hysteria to punish someone for acts which were not illegal at the time they were committed has not abated. After our Civil War, the State of Missouri enacted a law making it a crime to practice as a priest, a minister, deacon or elder of any religious sect or denomination, or to teach or preach or solemnize marriages unless one had taken an oath swearing he had not committed certain acts, even though such acts were legal at the time he committed them. Cummings, a priest of the Roman Catholic Church, followed his religious calling without taking the oath, and was convicted of a violation of the statute. The Supreme Court of the United States reversed the conviction and declared the statute unconstitutional as being ex post facto law. To illustrate how pervasive such laws can become in times of extreme passion, this same law applied to professors, teachers and lawyers. The Court pointed out that some of the acts condemned were not only legal but were also commendable at the time of their commission.

A bill of attainder is a legislative act which inflicts punishment without a judicial trial. One was passed as recently as 1943 when the House Un-American Activities Committee reported that the "views and philosophies" of three government workers made them unfit for government employment. The House of Representatives and then the Senate agreed, and ordered that employment of the three men be terminated and even that the salaries due them be not paid. Eventually the United States Supreme Court declared the law unconstitutional as a bill of attainder. The relationship of the prohibition against bills of attainder and the other provisions of the Bill of Rights is shown in this statement by Mr. Justice Black:

*. . . The Founders believed that punishment was too serious a matter to be entrusted to any*

152

*group other than an independent judiciary and a jury of twelve men acting on previously passed, unambiguous laws, with all the procedural safeguards they put in the Constitution as essential to a fair trial.*

A third relevant provision is to be found in the main body of the Constitution, Article VI, Clause 3:

*The Senators and Representatives before mentioned, and the Members of the several State Legislatures, and all executive and judicial Officers, both of the United States and of the several States, shall be bound by an Oath or Affirmation, to support this Constitution; but no religious Test shall ever be required as a Qualification to any Office or public Trust under the United States.*

One would suppose that this section is so precise and that by this time it would be so imbedded in our concept of constitutionalism that it would be inviolate. Yet, in 1961, the Supreme Court was obliged to invalidate a Maryland law which prohibited a man from becoming a notary public because he had declined to take an oath professing a belief in God.

Finally, the Constitution provides that the privilege of the writ of habeas corpus shall not be suspended unless, in cases of rebellion or invasion, the public safety may require it. The Great Writ, as it is often called, has been available through most of the history of the common law to give courts the power to investigate whether a man in custody is being held according to law. If he is not—that is, if he was wrongly confined in the first place, or if his treatment while being confined is unlawful—the court issues a writ of habeas corpus to release the man. It will be remembered, for example, that Bushnell and the other jurors who went to jail for refusing to convict William Penn were released on a writ of habeas corpus.

The writ is intimately related to the criminal provisions of the Bill of Rights; indeed, many of the important cases which define these rights began as petitions for writs of habeas corpus. Perhaps most important of all the functions of the Great Writ is its use to enforce the prohibition of the Eighth Amendment against "excessive bail." In particular, a person held without bail, or who has been imprisoned without charges being brought against him, can use habeas corpus to get a judicial hearing on whether his confinement is lawful. Many countries do not have such a procedure, so that a man can be arrested, jailed and never brought to trial.

When adopted, the first ten amendments were applicable only to the federal government; the states were not bound by them. But after the Civil War they were made applicable to the states through the "due process and equal protection" and the citizen-broadening clauses of the Fourteenth Amendment, the Thirteenth Amendment abolishing slavery and the Fifteenth Amendment guaranteeing the right to vote to everyone except women, who were belatedly given that right by the Nineteenth Amendment in 1920. The right of franchise is now open to all citizens and is inseparable in concept from our original Bill of Rights.

These are the great rights of Americans, and they buttress every freedom we enjoy. With them secure, we can go on to better things for everyone in the United States. Without them, we would go the way of other nations where the light of freedom has been extinguished.

# XII

## THE RESPONSIBLE
## CITIZEN

N O PEOPLE in history have made a more gal-
lant or more successful fight to preserve
their freedoms than the people of England in World
War II. When their army had been decimated in
France and almost trapped at Dunkirk by the vic-
torious panzer divisions of Hitler's army, the
English people rallied around their new Prime
Minister, Winston Churchill, who, in accepting
the office, promised them nothing but "blood,
sweat and tears."

The English accepted the burden. They saw
their great city of London and other industrial
centers bombed and burned with tens of thousands

dead and wounded. They broke up their families, sending their children to the open spaces to avoid extermination. They remained at work, living in bomb shelters, fighting fires, tending the wounded and burying the dead, until five years later the tide of war changed to victory.

In 1941, when the Battle of Britain was at its height, Winston Churchill visited Harrow, his old preparatory school, and spoke to the students. After praising them and the people of England for their perseverance in "such troubled times," he left them with this one uncompromising piece of advice:

*Never give in; never give in; never, never, never, never—in nothing great or small, large or petty—never give in except to convictions of honor and good sense. Never yield to force; never yield to the apparently overwhelming might of the enemy.*

Thus they maintained their nation with its freedoms strengthened because of the common sacrifices made in their defense. Throughout those horrifying years, the English were persevering, not just for their lives, but for their freedoms. They could have saved their lives by giving in to the Nazis, but it would have been without freedom. This they would not consider.

This determination preserved the freedoms of

Englishmen and should be an object lesson to everyone. Who loves freedom must guard it with tenacity.

Few Americans would doubt that we, like our English friends, would stand shoulder to shoulder and fight to the end, if it was necessary to protect our freedom. We are emotionally and materially prepared to resist such an assault. However, our geographic situation and our friendly relations with our neighbors diminish our concern about such an eventuality, and lead us to take the security of our freedoms for granted. This is a dangerous mistake, because as much freedom has been lost throughout history from internal neglect and erosion as from direct assault. There is always some crisis in life that can be seized upon to justify the abandonment of a portion of our freedom. At such times we might well heed the warning of Benjamin Franklin, given twenty years before our Bill of Rights:

*Those who would give up essential liberty to purchase a little temporary safety deserve neither liberty nor safety.*

Perhaps further light can be shed on how concerned citizens can be helpful in preserving our freedom, not only for ourselves but for those who are to follow us. We have talked at length about citizenship, its definition, and the manner in which it came into being, but we have not yet discussed some of its elements in detail and how they can best be exercised.

We need, and badly, the reestablishment of a moral tone for our nation: not blue laws, or censorship, or prohibition, but a national ethic which springs from the hearts and minds and actions of its citizens—one of open-mindedness which recognizes common decency, honesty and fair dealing in both public and private life.

We strive for these virtues in our family life, but we cannot hope to preserve them at home if they are negated in the neighborhood, the community or society generally. A nation cannot rise above the moral and cultural standards of its citizenry, and every thoughtful person must be aware that we have deteriorated in this respect in recent years. There has been a continuing erosion of standards which takes us constantly to lower levels.

For example, the increasing decadence of our theater, our films and the fiction we read is a matter of particular concern. All have deteriorated to such a degree that families are ashamed to share them together. Public success appears to be measured largely by the amount of obscenity in each. They become more degrading as time passes, while producers and writers continue to justify what they are doing by saying that they are merely satisfying the public demand, failing to recognize that they themselves whet the public appetite by salacious advertising and by creating works which trespass on community standards of frankness in the relations of the sexes. There is a considerable measure of truth in the pornographers' estimate of the marketplace for filth since they would hardly be producing in this vein if people were to withhold their patronage. Therein, of course, is the secret—eliminate the profit, and the traffic in such shoddy merchandise will vanish.

This is not to suggest government censorship. Censorship is a withering function and has been demonstrated throughout history to be dangerously oppressive. But pornographers should not be able to find it so easy to grow so rich through the abuse of the humanizing and edifying provisions of our Constitutional guarantee of freedom of speech and the press. Their excesses, widespread as they are, have also tainted the language we hear in the street, in the schools, from the public rostrum—and too often even in the privacy of the nation's living rooms.

We must have a moral and ethical awakening that will restore public and private language to generally accepted norms of decency. The dictionary definition of ethics is "The discipline dealing with what is good and bad or right and wrong or with moral duty and obligation." It embraces common honesty, compassion, tolerance, good manners and kindness, among many other virtues. It is that aspect of human nature which ultimately enables us to live together in harmony. It represents a force that can unite us into one great nation rather than divide us into contentious factions. It evokes the spirit which causes us to have concern for the well-being of others. We cannot live merely unto ourselves.

A nation is often appraised, particularly by strangers, by the manners that characterize the behavior of its people toward one another. While they were still on the way to Plymouth, the Pilgrims recognized this and enunciated a Code of Conduct, set down by John Winthrop. It would be difficult to improve on his simple formula:

*Wee must be knitt together in this worke as one man, wee must entertaine each other in brotherly Affeccion, wee must be willing to abridge our selues of our superfluities, for the supply of others necessities, wee must uphold a familiar Commerce together in a meekness, gentleness, patience and liberality, wee must delight in eache other, make others Condicions our owne, rejoyce together, mourne together, labour, and suffer together, allwayes haueing before our eyes our . . . Community. . . .*

These words must have made an impression on the colonists because some of the most observing visitors from other nations, including the Frenchman Alexis de Tocqueville, saw them borne out. De Tocqueville was fascinated by our easygoing civility and equality, and was of the opinion that it reflected the character of our people. During the Andrew Jackson era, an Englishwoman, Harriet Martineau, although often critical of us, had this to say of our manners:

*The manners of the Americans (in America) are the best I ever saw. . . . I believe it is not so much the outward plenty, or the mutual freedom, or the simplicity of manners, or the incessant play of humor, which characterize the whole people, as the sweet temper which is diffused over the land. They have been called the most good-tempered people in the world; and I think it must be so.*

She, too, felt American manners were not arbitrary conventions but instead reflected a genuine concern for others.

Lord Bryce, a few years before the turn of this century, in his great commentary, "The American Commonwealth," wrote that there was a naturalness about our manners, without condescension or false dignity, and that meeting as we

162

do on a simple and natural footing, there is more frankness and ease than is possible in other countries "where everyone is either looking up or looking down."

Other visitors have seen us through different eyes, and have not treated us so kindly. But the lesson to be learned from such observers, friendly or not, is that the manners of our nation are important and significant. In times of tension and stress manners usually break down, and the nation is surely in tension today. A spate of problems, foreign and domestic, press upon us. They are largely divisive and call for the exercise of great restraint if we are to refurbish our reputation for good manners. The tendency toward sharp rhetoric, polarization of views and intemperate actions is difficult to control. But our concern for the problems of the day should run deep, and our efforts to solve them should be vigorous. Both can be done, and done much better, through civility and reason rather than abrasiveness and intemperance.

Frustration is one of the major forces of our day. One would think that frustration would be the handmaid of stagnation instead of the consort of great change; yet the latter seems true today. There has been greater change in this century, through scientific and technological advances, than in any other comparable period in our history. Much has been done to relieve mankind of backbreaking work. Greater effort has been made to outlaw war as an instrument for solving disputes between nations. Standards of living have been raised in most parts of the world—certainly here in America. Greater concern has been shown for the poor and the sick. Education has been more highly developed and made more nearly universal. Improved means of communication have made the conveyance of news and information almost routine.

Yet in the face of these phenomenal changes, designed for the good of humanity, many here and abroad continue to be frustrated because these advances have not solved all our problems. And there is a residue of injurious side effects from many of our great achievements. Technology and automation, although bringing affluence to most of our people, have brought unemployment and poverty to large segments of our citizenry. Industry has polluted our environment. War and all that it entails has created inflation and an atmosphere of violence and despair. Advances in military weaponry pose a threat to the survival of mankind, accompanied by a surrender on the part of many to abject fear. Ever increasing mass production has tied the lives of millions to the humdrum life of the machine.

Scientific and technological advances, therefore, are accompanied by problems of such magnitude as to cause serious unrest among much of our population. It is imperative, therefore, that the greater our scientific and technological advances become, the more emphasis we should put on the importance of the individual and his relationship to the society in which these advances place him, and to the natural environment in which he must live.

If we are to prosper, we must believe in our institutions. Above all, we must believe in the basic document which protects all of our freedoms—the Constitution of the United States. The foundation of our society is the Constitution. It establishes our institutions, defines their procedures, limits the power of government, guarantees our rights as citizens, and imposes responsibilities on all of us commensurate with them.

This is not to say that the responsible citizen must agree with every "jot and tittle" of the Constitution as written by the Founding Fathers or as amended. They were wise men who realized that ours was an infant nation; that it was destined to grow and expand; that changing times and conditions would present new problems and call for changes in the Constitution if it was to endure through the ages. They did not intend to make the Constitution so rigid that changing conditions could only be met by destroying it.

One of the wisest things accomplished at the

Constitutional Convention was to construct the Constitution in broad general terms, and then make provision for amendment whenever the people, in their wisdom, should find it is needed. This power has been exercised twenty-five times in our national life, and other amendments are under serious consideration at present.

It is, therefore, necessary for responsible citizens to consider how effectively the Constitution is presently capable of meeting the needs of American life. Citizens have the right to change provisions of the Constitution and its administration as well. When they believe that changes in either would be in the interests of the nation, it becomes their duty to voice their desires. They have the right to dissent, in speech or in writing; to associate themselves with others for such a purpose; to petition the government; and to engage in the political process to accomplish the desired result. Such action demonstrates citizenship at its best. But it is essential that one act with prudence growing out of understanding. Emotional reforms are seldom helpful.

So it is not belief in or loyalty to the status quo that is essential to responsible citizenship. It cannot be overstated: we must believe in the purposes for which the government was created; the democratic processes by which those purposes can be achieved; and a commitment to an open society with individual liberty, political freedom and equal opportunity for every citizen.

We must believe in law because where there is no law there can be no freedom, particularly for the less advantaged members of society. When law breaks down, anarchy prevails. We must look at law, however, not only as an instrument of authority designed to punish but as a means of declaring what is right and prohibiting what is wrong to provide protection for every individual.

The responsible citizen does not live in isolation. He recognizes that he is a part of a community, a state and a nation, and that in playing his part he must act in relation to, and with consideration for, all others. His relation to his government, then, is not exclusive—it is shared with all others on an equal basis. That means that if we are to be useful none of us can be arbitrary and insist upon everything being done to our liking. There must be an underlying appreciation for the necessity of tolerance. As our Founding Fathers understood, even when our country was small and homespun in its way of life, there was a need for adjustment and compromise to bring the nation into being with a reasonable prospect of success. Now in our greatly enlarged society, every citizen must recognize the infinitely greater necessity to adjust his thoughts and actions to those of the community.

The problems of no two of the fifty states are

167

identical, nor are those of any two cities precisely the same, nor do urban and rural problems coincide. If every citizen or group should be adamant in demanding results strictly in accord with personal desires, the nation would be broken up into so many conflicting factions that consensus on anything would become impossible. We must, therefore, if we are to continue to have a viable government, consider yielding to the reasoning of others when it points the way toward accommodating the divergent groups which make up our body politic.

This is easy to prescribe, but it is one of the most difficult goals to achieve. Our own interests are so personal to each of us that it is often extremely difficult to appreciate a problem in the light of the interests of others as well. Yet, this is what we must do if we are to have a government "of the people, by the people, and for the people." This noble phrase, in more explicit language, means government of *all* the people, by *all* the people, and for *all* the people—as distinguished from of, by, or for *some* of the people.

I don't think this is overly idealistic or sentimental; and it is not merely political theory. It is pragmatism and enlightened self-interest at their best. It is something to which every citizen can and should lend a hand. At the risk of repetition, I suggest that if we are to fulfill our obligation as citizens, we must protect and preserve the free-

168

doms guaranteed by the Constitution and particularly those set forth in the Bill of Rights. They are what make us a free people.

There are neither rights nor freedoms in any meaningful sense unless they can be enjoyed by all. In their own countries the Nazis of Hitler had their rights; the Fascists of Mussolini had theirs; and the Communists of Stalin theirs. Yet millions in Germany, Italy and Russia died in concentration camps or purges or from other acts of sadistic cruelty. The important thing to remember is that in none of these nations were these cruelties put upon the people by foreign conquerors. They were initiated and executed by their own leaders when the people abandoned to them the unbridled power to rule. This mindless abandonment of power by the people was accorded in the belief that these tyrants would eliminate prevailing economic evils. Thus, it was the evasion of responsibility—not the subjugation by force—that led to the erosion of rights and, eventually, to cataclysmic disaster. I cannot help but recall the words of Mr. Justice Brandeis: "Those who won our independence believed . . . that the greatest menace to freedom is an inert people, that public discussion is a political duty and that this should be a fundamental principle of the American Government. . . . They eschewed silence coerced by law."

No, the democratic way of life is not easy. It

conveys great privileges, but constant vigilance is needed to preserve them. This vigilance must be maintained by those responsible for the government; and in our country those responsible are "we, the people"—no one else. Responsible citizenship is, therefore, the sheet anchor of our Republic. With it, we can withstand the storm; without it we are helplessly at sea. It is beyond question the ingredient Benjamin Franklin had in mind when he said, "A republic, if you can keep it."

# APPENDIX I

# The Declaration of Independence

THE DECLARATION OF INDEPENDENCE which preceded the Constitution bespeaks the spirit of our institutions and our aspirations for the future. While the Constitution, as originally written and later amended, defines the rights and responsibilities of citizenship, the Declaration of Independence proclaims to the world as well as to Americans our concept "That all men are created equal, that they are endowed by their Creator with certain unalienable rights, that among these are life, liberty and the pursuit of happiness." And as assurance of the sincerity of this Declaration, the signers "mutually pledge[d] to each other our lives, our fortune and our sacred honor."

E. W.

IN CONGRESS, JULY 4, 1776

## A DECLARATION

BY THE REPRESENTATIVES OF THE

UNITED STATES OF AMERICA,

IN GENERAL CONGRESS ASSEMBLED.

WHEN in the Course of human Events, it becomes necessary for one People to dissolve the Political Bands which have connected them with another, and to assume among the Powers of the Earth, the separate and equal Station to which the Laws of Nature and of Nature's God entitle them, a decent

Respect to the Opinions of Mankind requires that they should declare the causes which impel them to the Separation.

WE hold these Truths to be self-evident, that all Men are created equal, that they are endowed by their Creator with certain unalienable Rights, that among these are Life, Liberty, and the Pursuit of Happiness—That to secure these Rights, Governments are instituted among Men, deriving their just Powers from the Consent of the Governed, that whenever any Form of Government becomes destructive of these Ends, it is the Right of the People to alter or to abolish it, and to institute new Government, laying its Foundation on such Principles, and organizing its Powers in such Form, as to them shall seem most likely to effect their Safety and Happiness. Prudence, indeed, will dictate that Governments long established should not be changed for light and transient Causes; and accordingly all Experience hath shewn, that Mankind are more disposed to suffer, while Evils are sufferable, than to right themselves by abolishing the Forms to which they are accustomed. But when a long Train of Abuses and Usurpations, pursuing invariably the same Object, evinces a Design to reduce them under absolute Despotism, it is their Right, it is their Duty, to throw off such Government, and to provide new Guards for their future Security. Such has been the patient Sufferance of these Colonies; and such is now the Necessity which constrains them to alter their former Systems of Government. The History of the present King of Great-Britain is a History of repeated Injuries and Usurpations, all having in direct Object the Establishment of an absolute Tyranny over these States. To prove this, let Facts be submitted to a candid World.

HE has refused his Assent to Laws, the most wholesome and necessary for the public Good.

HE has forbidden his Governors to pass Laws of immediate and pressing Importance, unless suspended in their Operation till his Assent should be obtained; and when so suspended, he has utterly neglected to attend to them.

HE has refused to pass other Laws for the Accommodation of large Districts of People, unless those People would relinquish the Right of Representation in the Legislature, a Right inestimable to them, and formidable to Tyrants only.

HE has called together Legislative Bodies at Places unusual, uncomfortable, and distant from the Depository of their public Records, for the sole Purpose of fatiguing them into Compliance with his Measures.

HE has dissolved Representative Houses repeatedly, for opposing with manly Firmness his Invasions on the Rights of the People.

HE has refused for a long Time, after such Dissolutions, to cause others to be elected; whereby the Legislative Powers, incapable of Annihilation, have returned to the People at large for their exercise; the State remaining in the mean time exposed to all the Dangers of Invasion from without, and Convulsions within.

HE has endeavoured to prevent the Population of these States; for that Purpose obstructing the Laws for Naturalization of Foreigners; refusing to pass others to encourage their Migrations hither, and raising the Conditions of new Appropriations of Lands.

HE has obstructed the Administration of Justice, by refusing his Assent to Laws for establishing Judiciary Powers.

HE has made Judges dependent on his Will alone, for the Tenure of their Offices, and the Amount and Payment of their Salaries.

HE has erected a Multitude of new Offices, and sent hither Swarms of Officers to harass our People, and eat out their Substance.

HE has kept among us, in Times of Peace, Standing Armies, without the consent of our Legislatures.

HE has affected to render the Military independent of and superior to the Civil Power.

HE has combined with others to subject us to a Jurisdiction foreign to our Constitution, and unacknowledged by our Laws; giving his Assent to their Acts of pretended Legislation:

FOR quartering large Bodies of Armed Troops among us:

FOR protecting them, by a mock Trial, from Punishment for any Murders which they should commit on the Inhabitants of these States:

FOR cutting off our Trade with all Parts of the World:

FOR imposing Taxes on us without our Consent:

FOR depriving us, in many Cases, of the Benefits of Trial by Jury:

For transporting us beyond Seas to be tried for pretended Offences:

For abolishing the free System of English Laws in a neighbouring Province, establishing therein an arbitrary Government, and enlarging its Boundaries, so as to render it at once an Example and fit Instrument for introducing the same absolute Rule into these Colonies:

For taking away our Charters, abolishing our most valuable Laws, and altering fundamentally the Forms of our Governments:

For suspending our own Legislatures, and declaring themselves invested with Power to legislate for us in all Cases whatsoever.

He has abdicated Government here, by declaring us out of his Protection and waging War against us.

He has plundered our Seas, ravaged our Coasts, burnt our Towns, and destroyed the Lives of our People.

He is, at this Time, transporting large Armies of foreign Mercenaries to compleat the Works of Death, Desolation, and Tyranny, already begun with circumstances of Cruelty and Perfidy, scarcely parallelled in the most barbarous Ages, and totally unworthy the Head of a civilized Nation.

He has constrained our fellow Citizens taken Captive on the high Seas to bear Arms against their Country, to become the Executioners of their Friends and Brethren, or to fall themselves by their Hands.

He has excited domestic Insurrections amongst us, and has endeavoured to bring on the Inhabitants of our Frontiers, the merciless Indian Savages, whose known Rule of Warfare, is an undistinguished Destruction of all Ages, Sexes and Conditions.

In every stage of these Oppressions we have Petitioned for Redress in the most humble Terms: Our repeated Petitions have been answered only by repeated Injury. A Prince, whose Character is thus marked by every act which may define a Tyrant, is unfit to be the Ruler of a free People.

Nor have we been wanting in Attentions to our British Brethren. We have warned them from Time to Time of Attempts by their Legislature to extend an unwarrantable Jurisdiction over us. We have reminded them of the Circumstances of our Emigration and Settlement here. We have appealed to their native Justice and Magnanimity, and we have conjured them by the Ties of our common Kindred to disavow these Usurpations, which, would inevitably interrupt our Connections and Correspondence. They too have been deaf to the Voice of Justice and of Consanguinity. We must, there, acquiesce in the Necessity, which denounces our Separation, and hold them, as we hold the rest of Mankind, Enemies in War, in Peace, Friends.

WE, therefore, the Representatives of the UNITED STATES OF AMERICA, in GENERAL CONGRESS, Assembled, appealing to the Supreme Judge of the World for the Rectitude of our Intentions, do, in the Name, and by Authority of the good People of these Colonies, solemnly Publish and Declare, That these United Colonies are, and of Right ought to be, FREE AND INDEPENDENT STATES; that they are absolved from all Allegiance to the British Crown, and that all political Connection between them and the State of Great-Britain, is and ought to be totally dissolved; and that as FREE AND INDEPENDENT STATES, they have full Power to levy War, conclude Peace, contract Alliances, establish Commerce, and to do all other Acts and Things which INDEPENDENT STATES may of right do. And for the support of this Declaration, with a firm Reliance on the Protection of divine Providence, we mutually pledge to each other our Lives, our Fortunes, and our sacred Honor.

*Signed by* ORDER *and in*
BEHALF *of the* CONGRESS,
JOHN HANCOCK, PRESIDENT

ATTEST.

CHARLES THOMSON, SECRETARY.

JOHN ADAMS [Lawyer/age 40], SAMUEL ADAMS [Politician/53], JOSIAH BARTLETT [Physician/46], CARTER BRAXTON [Planter/39], CHARLES CARROLL [Planter/38], SAMUEL CHASE [Lawyer/35], ABRAHAM CLARK [Lawyer-Farmer/40], GEORGE CLYMER [Merchant/37], WILLIAM ELLERY [Lawyer/48], WILLIAM FLOYD [Farmer/41], BENJAMIN FRANKLIN [Public servant/70], ELBRIDGE GERRY [Merchant/31], BUTTON GWINNETT [Planter/c. 41], LYMAN HALL [Physician/52], JOHN HANCOCK [Merchant/39], BENJAMIN HARRISON [Planter/c. 50], JOHN HART [Farmer/c. 65], JOSEPH HEWES [Merchant/46], THOMAS HEYWARD [Lawyer/29], WILLIAM HOOPER [Lawyer/34], STEPHEN HOPKINS [Public servant/71], FRANCIS HOPKINSON [Lawyer/38], SAMUEL HUNTINGTON [Lawyer/45], THOMAS JEFFERSON [Lawyer-Planter/33], RICHARD HENRY LEE [Planter/

177

44], FRANCIS LIGHTFOOT LEE [Planter/41], FRANCIS LEWIS [Merchant/ 63], PHILIP LIVINGSTON [Merchant/60], THOMAS LYNCH [Planter/26], THOMAS MCKEAN [Lawyer/42], ARTHUR MIDDLETON [Planter/34], LEWIS MORRIS [Landowner/50], ROBERT MORRIS [Merchant/42], JOHN MORTON [Surveyor/c. 42], THOMAS NELSON [Planter/41], WILLIAM PACA [Lawyer/ 37], ROBERT TREAT PAINE [Lawyer/45], JOHN PENN [Lawyer/c. 36], GEORGE READ [Lawyer/42], CAESAR RODNEY [Landowner/48], GEORGE ROSS [Lawyer/46], BENJAMIN RUSH [Physician/30], EDWARD RUTLEDGE [Lawyer/26], ROGER SHERMAN [Merchant/55], JAMES SMITH [Lawyer-Iron master/c. 57], RICHARD STOCKTON [Lawyer/46], THOMAS STONE [Lawyer-Planter/c. 33], GEORGE TAYLOR [Iron master/c. 60], MATTHEW THORNTON [Physician/62], GEORGE WALTON [Lawyer/c. 35], WILLIAM WHIPPLE [Merchant/46], WILLIAM WILLIAMS [Public servant-Merchant/ 45], JAMES WILSON [Lawyer/33], JOHN WITHERSPOON [College president-Clergyman /53], OLIVER WOLCOTT [Lawyer/49], GEORGE WYTHE [Lawyer/50].

# APPENDIX II

# The Constitution
# of the United States

WE, THE PEOPLE of the United States, in order to form a more perfect union, establish justice, insure domestic tranquility, provide for the common defence, promote the general welfare, and secure the blessing of liberty to ourselves and our posterity, do ordain and establish this Constitution for the United States of America.

## ARTICLE I

*Sect.* 1. ALL legislative powers herein granted shall be vested in a Congress of the United States, which shall consist of a Senate and House of Representatives.

*Sect.* 2. The House of Representatives shall be composed of members chosen every second year by the people of the several states, and the electors in each state shall have the qualifications requisite for electors of the most numerous branch of the state legislature.

No person shall be a representative who shall not have attained to the age of twenty-five years, and been seven years a citizen of the United States, and who shall not, when elected, be an inhabitant of that state in which he shall be chosen.

\* **[Representatives and direct taxes shall be apportioned among the several states which may be included within this Union, according to their respective numbers, which shall be determined by adding to the whole number of free persons, including those bound to service for a term of years, and excluding Indians not taxed, three-fifths of all other persons.]**

---

\* The part enclosed by brackets was amended by section 2 of Article XIV.

The actual enumeration shall be made within three years after the first meeting of the Congress of the United States, and within every subsequent term of ten years, in such manner as they shall by law direct. The number of representatives shall not exceed one for every thirty thousand, but each state shall have at least one representative; and until such enumeration shall be made, the state of New-Hampshire shall be entitled to chuse three, Massachusetts eight, Rhode-Island and Providence Plantations one, Connecticut five, New-York six, New-Jersey four, Pennsylvania eight, Delaware one, Maryland six, Virginia ten, North-Carolina five, South-Carolina five, and Georgia three.

When vacancies happen in the representation from any state, the Executive authority thereof shall issue writs of election to fill such vacancies.

The House of Representatives shall chuse their Speaker and other officers; and shall have the sole power of impeachment.

*Sect.* 3. The Senate of the United States shall be composed of two senators from each state, ** **[chosen by the legislature thereof,]** for six years; and each senator shall have one vote.

Immediately after they shall be assembled in consequence of the first election, they shall be divided as equally as may be into three classes. The seats of the senators of the first class shall be vacated at the expiration of the second year, of the second class at the expiration of the fourth year, and of the third class at the expiration of the sixth year, so that one-third may be chosen every second year; **[and if vacancies happen by resignation, or otherwise, during the recess of the Legislature of any state, the Executive thereof may make temporary appointments until the next meeting of the Legislature, which shall then fill such vacancies.]**

No person shall be a senator who shall not have attained to the age of thirty years, and been nine years a citizen of the United States, and who shall not, when elected, be an inhabitant of that state for which he shall be chosen.

The Vice-President of the United States shall be President

** The clause enclosed by brackets was amended by clause i of Article XVII.

of the Senate, but shall have no vote, unless they be equally divided.

The Senate shall chuse their other officers, and also a President pro tempore, in the absence of the Vice-President, or when he shall exercise the office of President of the United States.

The Senate shall have the sole power to try all impeachments. When sitting for that purpose, they shall be on oath or affirmation. When the President of the United States is tried, the Chief Justice shall preside: And no person shall be convicted without the concurrence of two-thirds of the members present.

Judgment in cases of impeachment shall not extend further than to removal from office and disqualification to hold and enjoy any office of honor, trust or profit under the United States; but the party convicted shall nevertheless be liable and subject to indictment, trial, judgment and punishment, according to law.

*Sect.* 4. The times, places and manner of holding elections for senators and representatives, shall be prescribed in each state by the legislature thereof; but the Congress may at any time by law make or alter such regulations, except as to the places of chusing Senators.

The Congress shall assemble at least once in every year, and such meeting shall **[be on the first Monday in December,]** unless they shall by law appoint a different day.

*Sect.* 5. Each house shall be the judge of the elections, returns and qualifications of its own members, and a majority of each shall constitute a quorum to do business; but a smaller number may adjourn from day to day, and may be authorized to compel the attendance of absent members, in such manner, and under such penalties as each house may provide.

Each house may determine the rules of its proceedings, punish its members for disorderly behaviour, and, with the concurrence of two-thirds, expel a member.

Each house shall keep a journal of its proceedings, and from time to time publish the same, excepting such parts as may in their judgment require secrecy; and the yeas and nays of the members of either house on any question shall, at the desire of one-fifth of those present, be entered on the journal.

Neither house, during the session of Congress shall, without the consent of the other, adjourn for more than three days, nor to any other place than that in which the two houses shall be sitting.

*Sect.* 6. The senators and representatives shall receive a compensation for their services, to be ascertained by law, and paid out of the treasury of the United States. They shall in all cases, except treason, felony and breach of the peace, be privileged from arrest during their attendance at the session of their respective houses, and in going to and returning from the same; and for any speech or debate in either house, they shall not be questioned in any other place.

No senator or representative shall, during the time for which he was elected, be appointed to any civil office under the authority of the United States, which shall have been created, or the emoluments whereof shall have been encreased during such time; and no person holding any office under the United States, shall be a member of either house during his continuance in office.

*Sect.* 7. All bills for raising revenue shall originate in the house of representatives; but the senate may propose or concur with amendments as on other bills.

Every bill which shall have passed the house of representatives and the senate, shall, before it becomes a law, be presented to the president of the United States; if he approve he shall sign it, but if not he shall return it, with his objections to that house in which it shall have originated, who shall enter the objections at large on their journal, and proceed to reconsider it. If after such reconsideration two-thirds of that house shall agree to pass the bill, it shall be sent, together with the objections, to the other house, by which it shall likewise be reconsidered, and if approved by two-thirds of that house, it shall become a law. But in all such cases the votes of both houses shall be determined by yeas and nays, and the names of the persons voting for and against the bill shall be entered on the journal of each house respectively. If any bill shall not be returned by the President within ten days (Sundays excepted) after it shall have been presented to him, the same shall be a law, in like manner as if he had signed it, unless the Congress by their adjournment prevent its return, in which case it shall not be a law.

Every order, resolution, or vote to which the concurrence

of the Senate and House of Representatives may be necessary (except on a question of adjournment) shall be presented to the President of the United States; and before the same shall take effect, shall be approved by him, or, being disapproved by him, shall be repassed by two-thirds of the Senate and House of Representatives, according to the rules and limitations prescribed in the case of a bill.

*Sect.* 8. The Congress shall have power

To lay and collect taxes, duties, imposts and excises, to pay the debts and provide for the common defence and general welfare of the United States; but all duties, imposts and excises shall be uniform throughout the United States;

To borrow money on the credit of the United States;

To regulate commerce with foreign nations, and among the several states, and with the Indian tribes;

To establish an uniform rule of naturalization, and uniform laws on the subject of bankruptcies throughout the United States;

To coin money, regulate the value thereof, and of foreign coin, and fix the standard of weights and measures;

To provide for the punishment of counterfeiting the securities and current coin of the United States;

To establish post offices and post roads;

To promote the progress of science and useful arts, by securing for limited times to authors and inventors the exclusive right to their respective writings and discoveries;

To constitute tribunals inferior to the supreme court;

To define and punish piracies and felonies committed on the high seas, and offences against the law of nations;

To declare war, grant letters of marque and reprisal, and make rules concerning captures on land and water;

To raise and support armies, but no appropriation of money to that use shall be for a longer term than two years;

To provide and maintain a navy;

To make rules for the government and regulation of the land and naval forces;

To provide for calling forth the militia to execute the laws of the union, suppress insurrections and repel invasions;

To provide for organizing, arming, and disciplining, the militia, and for governing such part of them as may be employed in the service of the United States, reserving to the

States respectively, the appointment of the officers, and the authority of training the militia according to the discipline prescribed by Congress;

To exercise exclusive legislation in all cases whatsoever, over such district (not exceeding ten miles square) as may, by cession of particular States, and the acceptance of Congress, become the seat of the government of the United States, and to exercise like authority over all places purchased by the consent of the legislature of the states in which the same shall be, for the erection of forts, magazines, arsenals, dock-yards, and other needful buildings;—And

To make all laws which shall be necessary and proper for carrying into execution the foregoing powers, and all other powers vested by this constitution in the government of the United States, or in any department or officer thereof.

*Sect.* 9. The migration or importation of such persons as any of the states now existing shall think proper to admit, shall not be prohibited by the Congress prior to the year one thousand eight hundred and eight, but a tax or duty may be imposed on such importation, not exceeding ten dollars for each person.

The privilege of the writ of habeas corpus shall not be suspended, unless when in cases of rebellion or invasion the public safety may require it.

No bill of attainder or ex post facto law shall be passed.

No capitation, or other direct, tax shall be laid, unless in proportion to the census or enumeration herein before directed to be taken.

No tax or duty shall be laid on articles exported from any state. No preference shall be given by any regulation of commerce or revenue to the ports of one state over those of another: nor shall vessels bound to, or from, one state, be obliged to enter, clear, or pay duties in another.

No money shall be drawn from the treasury, but in consequence of appropriations made by law; and a regular statement and account of the receipts and expenditures of all public money shall be published from time to time.

No title of nobility shall be granted by the United States: —And no person holding any office of profit or trust under them, shall, without the consent of the Congress, accept of any

186

present, emolument, office, or title, of any kind whatever, from any king, prince, or foreign state.

*Sect.* 10. No state shall enter into any treaty, alliance, or confederation; grant letters of marque and reprisal; coin money; emit bills of credit; make any thing but gold and silver coin a tender in payment of debts; pass any bill of attainder, ex post facto law, or law impairing the obligation of contracts, or grant any title of nobility.

No state shall, without the consent of the Congress, lay any imposts or duties on imports or exports, except what may be absolutely necessary for executing its inspection laws; and the net produce of all duties and imposts, laid by any state on imports or exports, shall be for the use of the Treasury of the United States; and all such laws shall be subject to the revision and control of the Congress. No state shall, without the consent of Congress, lay any duty of tonnage, keep troops, or ships of war in time of peace, enter into any agreement or compact with another state, or with a foreign power, or engage in war, unless actually invaded, or in such imminent danger as will not admit of delay.

## ARTICLE II

*Sect.* 1. The executive power shall be vested in a president of the United States of America. He shall hold his office during the term of four years, and, together with the vice-president, chosen for the same term, be elected as follows.

Each state shall appoint, in such manner as the legislature thereof may direct, a number of electors, equal to the whole number of senators and representatives to which the state may be entitled in the Congress: but no senator or representative, or person holding an office of trust or profit under the United States, shall be appointed an elector.

**[The electors shall meet in their respective states, and vote by ballot for two persons, of whom one at least shall not be an inhabitant of the same state with themselves. And they shall make a list of all the persons voted for, and of the number of votes for each; which list they shall sign and certify, and transmit sealed to the seat of the government of the United States, directed to the president of the senate. The president of**

the senate shall, in the presence of the senate and house of representatives, open all the certificates, and the votes shall then be counted. The person having the greatest number of votes shall be the president, if such number be a majority of the whole number of electors appointed; and if there be more than one who have such majority, and have an equal number of votes, then the house of representatives shall immediately chuse by ballot one of them for president; and if no person have a majority, then from the five highest on the list the said house shall in like manner chuse the president. But in chusing the president, the votes shall be taken by states, the representation from each state having one vote; a quorum for this purpose shall consist of a member or members from two-thirds of the states, and a majority of all the states shall be necessary to a choice. In every case, after the choice of the president, the person having the greatest number of votes of the electors shall be the vice-president. But if there should remain two or more who have equal votes, the senate shall chuse from them by ballot the vice-president.]

The Congress may determine the time of chusing the electors, and the day on which they shall give their votes; which day shall be the same throughout the United States.

No person except a natural born citizen, or a citizen of the United States, at the time of the adoption of this constitution, shall be eligible to the office of president; neither shall any person be eligible to that office who shall not have attained to the age of thirty-five years, and been fourteen years a resident within the United States.

In case of the removal of the president from office, or of his death, resignation, or inability to discharge the powers and duties of the said office, the same shall devolve on the vice-president, and the Congress may by law provide for the case of removal, death, resignation or inability, both of the president and vice-president, declaring what officer shall then act as president, and such officer shall act accordingly, until the disability be removed, or a president be elected.

The president shall, at stated times, receive for his services, a compensation, which shall neither be increased nor diminished during the period for which he shall have been elected, and he shall not receive within that period any other emolument from the United States, or any of them.

Before he enter on the execution of his office, he shall take the following oath or affirmation:

"I do solemnly swear (or affirm) that I will faithfully execute the office of president of the United States, and will to the best of my ability, preserve, protect and defend the constitution of the United States."

*Sect.* 2. The president shall be commander in chief of the army and navy of the United States, and of the militia of the several States, when called into the actual service of the United States; he may require the opinion, in writing, of the principal officer in each of the executive departments, upon any subject relating to the duties of their respective offices, and he shall have power to grant reprieves and pardons for offences against the United States, except in cases of impeachment.

He shall have power, by and with the advice and consent of the senate, to make treaties, provided two-thirds of the senators present concur; and he shall nominate, and by and with the advice and consent of the senate, shall appoint ambassadors, other public ministers and consuls, judges of the supreme court, and all other officers of the United States, whose appointments are not herein otherwise provided for, and which shall be established by law. But the Congress may by law vest the appointment of such inferior officers, as they think proper, in the president alone, in the courts of law, or in the heads of departments.

The president shall have power to fill up all vacancies that may happen during the recess of the senate, by granting commissions which shall expire at the end of their session.

*Sect.* 3. He shall from time to time give to the Congress information of the state of the union, and recommend to their consideration such measures as he shall judge necessary and expedient; he may, on extraordinary occasions, convene both houses, or either of them, and in case of disagreement between them, with respect to the time of adjournment, he may adjourn them to such time as he shall think proper; he shall receive ambassadors and other public ministers; he shall take care that the laws be faithfully executed, and shall commission all the officers of the United States.

*Sect.* 4. The president, vice-president and all civil officers of the United States, shall be removed from office on impeachment for, and conviction of, treason, bribery, or other high crimes and misdemeanors.

## ARTICLE III

*Sect.* 1. The judicial power of the United States, shall be vested in one supreme court, and in such inferior courts as the Congress may from time to time ordain and establish. The judges, both of the supreme and inferior courts, shall hold their offices during good behaviour, and shall, at stated times, receive for their services, a compensation, which shall not be diminished during their continuance in office.

*Sect.* 2. The judicial power shall extend to all cases, in law and equity, arising under this constitution, the laws of the United States, and treaties made, or which shall be made, under their authority; to all cases of admiralty and maritime jurisdiction; to controversies to which the United States shall be a party; to controversies between two or more States, between a state and citizens of another state, between citizens of different States, between citizens of the same state claiming lands under grants of different States, and between a state, or the citizens thereof, and foreign States, citizens or subjects.

In all cases affecting ambassadors, other public ministers and consuls, and those in which a state shall be party, the supreme court shall have original jurisdiction. In all the other cases before mentioned, the supreme court shall have appellate jurisdiction, both as to law and fact, with such exceptions, and under such regulations as the Congress shall make.

The trial of all crimes, except in cases of impeachment, shall be by jury; and such trial shall be held in the state where the said crimes shall have been committed; but when not committed within any state, the trial shall be at such place or places as the Congress may by law have directed.

*Sect.* 3. Treason against the United States, shall consist only in levying war against them, or in adhering to their enemies, giving them aid and comfort. No person shall be convicted of treason unless on the testimony of two witnesses to the same overt act, or on confession in open court.

The Congress shall have power to declare the punishment of treason, but no attainder of treason shall work corruption of blood, or forfeiture except during the life of the person attainted.

## ARTICLE IV

*Sect.* 1. Full faith and credit shall be given in each state to the public acts, records, and judicial proceedings of every other state. And the Congress may by general laws prescribe the manner in which such acts, records and proceedings shall be proved, and the effect thereof.

*Sect.* 2. The citizens of each state shall be entitled to all privileges and immunities of citizens in the several states.

A person charged in any state with treason, felony, or other crime, who shall flee from justice, and be found in another state, shall, on demand of the executive authority of the state from which he fled, be delivered up, to be removed to the state having jurisdiction of the crime.

\* **[No person held to service or labour in one state, under the laws thereof, escaping into another, shall, in consequence of any law or regulation therein, be discharged from such service or labour, but shall be delivered up on claim of the party to whom such service or labour may be due.]**

*Sect.* 3. New states may be admitted by the Congress into this union; but no new state shall be formed or erected within the jurisdiction of any other state; nor any state be formed by the junction of two or more states, or parts of states, without the consent of the legislatures of the states concerned as well as of the Congress.

The Congress shall have power to dispose of and make all needful rules and regulations respecting the territory or other property belonging to the United States; and nothing in this Constitution shall be so construed as to prejudice any claims of the United States, or of any particular state.

*Sect.* 4. The United States shall guarantee to every state in this union a Republican form of government, and shall protect each of them against invasion; and on application of the legislature, or of the executive (when the legislature cannot be convened) against domestic violence.

## ARTICLE V

The Congress, whenever two-thirds of both houses shall deem it necessary, shall propose amendments to this consti-

---

\* Superseded by Article XIII.

tution, or, on the application of the legislatures of two-thirds of the several states, shall call a convention for proposing amendments, which, in either case, shall be valid to all intents and purposes, as part of this constitution, when ratified by the legislatures of three-fourths of the several states, or by conventions in three-fourths thereof, as the one or the other mode of ratification may be proposed by Congress; Provided, that no amendment which may be made prior to the year one thousand eight hundred and eight shall in any manner affect the first and fourth clauses in the ninth section of the first article; and that no state, without its consent, shall be deprived of its equal suffrage in the senate.

## ARTICLE VI

All debts contracted and engagements entered into, before the adoption of this Constitution, shall be as valid against the United States under this Constitution, as under the confederation.

This constitution, and the laws of the United States which shall be made in pursuance thereof; and all treaties made, or which shall be made, under the authority of the United States, shall be the supreme law of the land; and the judges in every state shall be bound thereby, any thing in the constitution or laws of any state to the contrary notwithstanding.

The senators and representatives beforementioned, and the members of the several state legislatures, and all executive and judicial officers, both of the United States and of the several States, shall be bound by oath or affirmation, to support this constitution; but no religious test shall ever be required as a qualification to any office or public trust under the United States.

## ARTICLE VII

The ratification of the conventions of nine States, shall be sufficient for the establishment of this constitution between the States so ratifying the same.

[*Done in Convention, by the unanimous consent of the States present, the seventeenth day of September, in the year of our Lord one thousand seven hundred and eighty-seven, and of the Independence of the United States of America the twelfth. In witness whereof we have hereunto subscribed our Names.*]

# THE CONSTITUTIONAL AMENDMENTS

The first ten amendments to the original Constitution are known as the Bill of Rights.

### AMENDMENT I

Congress shall make no law respecting an establishment of religion, or prohibiting the free exercise thereof; or abridging the freedom of speech, or of the press; or the right of the people peaceably to assemble, and to petition the Government for a redress of grievances.

### AMENDMENT II

A well regulated Militia, being necessary to the security of a free State, the right of the people to keep and bear Arms, shall not be infringed.

### AMENDMENT III

No Soldier shall, in time of peace be quartered in any house, without the consent of the Owner, nor in time of war, but in a manner to be prescribed by law.

### AMENDMENT IV

The right of the people to be secure in their persons, houses, papers, and effects, against unreasonable searches and seizures, shall not be violated, and no Warrants shall issue, but upon probable cause, supported by Oath or affirmation, and particularly describing the place to be searched, and the persons or things to be seized.

### AMENDMENT V

No person shall be held to answer for a capital, or otherwise infamous crime, unless on a presentment or indictment of a Grand Jury, except in cases arising in the land or naval forces, or in the Militia, when in actual service in time of War or public danger; nor shall any person be subject for the same offence to be twice put in jeopardy of life or limb; nor shall be compelled in any criminal case to be a witness against himself, nor be deprived of life, liberty, or property, without due process of law; nor shall private property be taken for public use, without just compensation.

### AMENDMENT VI

In all criminal prosecutions, the accused shall enjoy the right to a speedy and public trial, by an impartial jury of the State and district wherein the crime shall have been committed, which district shall have been previously ascertained by law, and to be informed of the nature and cause of the accusation; to be confronted with the witnesses against him; to have compulsory process for obtaining witnesses in his favor, and to have the Assistance of Counsel for his defence.

### AMENDMENT VII

In Suits at common law, where the value in controversy shall exceed twenty dollars, the right of trial by jury shall be preserved, and no fact tried by a jury, shall be otherwise re-examined in any Court of the United States, than according to the rules of the common law.

### AMENDMENT VIII

Excessive bail shall not be required, nor excessive fines imposed, nor cruel and unusual punishments inflicted.

### AMENDMENT IX

The enumeration in the Constitution, of certain rights, shall not be construed to deny or disparage others retained by the people.

### AMENDMENT X

The powers not delegated to the United States by the Constitution, nor prohibited by it to the States, are reserved to the States respectively, or to the people.

### AMENDMENT XI

The Judicial power of the United States shall not be construed to extend to any suit in law or equity, commenced or prosecuted against one of the United States by Citizens of another State, or by Citizens or Subjects of any Foreign State.

### AMENDMENT XII

The Electors shall meet in their respective states, and vote by ballot for President and Vice-President, one of whom, at least, shall not be an inhabitant of the same state with themselves; they shall name in their ballots the person voted for as President, and in distinct ballots the person voted for as Vice-President, and they shall make distinct lists of all persons voted for as President, and of all persons voted for as Vice-President, and of the number of votes for each, which lists they shall sign and certify, and transmit sealed to the seat of the government of the United States, directed to the President of the Senate;—The President of the Senate shall, in the presence of the Senate and House of Representatives, open all the certificates and the votes shall then be counted;—

The person having the greatest number of votes for President, shall be the President, if such number be a majority of the whole number of Electors appointed; and if no person have such majority, then from the persons having the highest numbers not exceeding three on the list of those voted for as President, the House of Representatives shall choose immediately, by ballot, the President. But in choosing the President, the votes shall be taken by states, the representation from each state having one vote; a quorum for this purpose shall consist of a member or members from two-thirds of the states, and a majority of all the states shall be necessary to a choice. **\*[And if the House of Representatives shall not choose a President whenever the right of choice shall devolve upon them, before the fourth day of March next following, then the Vice-President shall act as President, as in the case of the death or other constitutional disability of the President.]** —The person having the greatest number of votes as Vice-President, shall be the Vice-President, if such number be a majority of the whole number of Electors appointed, and if no person have a majority, then from the two highest numbers on the list, the Senate shall choose the Vice-President; a quorum for the purpose shall consist of two-thirds of the whole number of Senators, and a majority of the whole number shall be necessary to a choice. But no person constitutionally ineligible to the office of President shall be eligible to that of Vice-President of the United States.

## AMENDMENT XIII

Section 1. Neither slavery nor involuntary servitude, except as a punishment for crime whereof the party shall have been duly convicted, shall exist within the United States, or any place subject to their jurisdiction.

Section 2. Congress shall have power to enforce this article by appropriate legislation.

## AMENDMENT XIV

Section 1. All persons born or naturalized in the United States, and subject to the jurisdiction thereof, are citizens of the United States and of the State wherein they reside. No State shall make or enforce any law which shall abridge the

---

\*The part enclosed by brackets has been superseded by section 3 of Article XX.

privileges or immunities of citizens of the United States; nor shall any State deprive any person of life, liberty, or property, without due process of law; nor deny to any person within its jurisdiction the equal protection of the laws.

Section 2. Representatives shall be apportioned among the several States according to their respective numbers, counting the whole number of persons in each State, excluding Indians not taxed. But when the right to vote at any election for the choice of electors for President and Vice-President of the United States, Representatives in Congress, the Executive and Judicial officers of a State, or the members of the Legislature thereof, is denied to any of the male inhabitants of such State, being twenty-one years of age, and citizens of the United States, or in any way abridged, except for participation in rebellion, or other crime, the basis of representation therein shall be reduced in the proportion which the number of such male citizens shall bear to the whole number of male citizens twenty-one years of age in such State.

Section 3. No person shall be a Senator or Representative in Congress, or elector of President and Vice-President, or hold any office, civil or military, under the United States, or under any State, who, having previously taken an oath, as a member of Congress, or as an officer of the United States, or as a member of any State legislature, or as an executive or judicial officer of any State, to support the Constitution of the United States, shall have engaged in insurrection or rebellion against the same, or given aid or comfort to the enemies thereof. But Congress may by a vote of two-thirds of each House, remove such disability.

Section 4. The validity of the public debt of the United States, authorized by law, including debts incurred for payment of pensions and bounties for services in suppressing insurrection or rebellion, shall not be questioned. But neither the United States nor any State shall assume or pay any debt or obligation incurred in aid of insurrection or rebellion against the United States, or any claim for the loss or emancipation of any slave; but all such debts, obligations and claims shall be held illegal and void.

Section 5. The Congress shall have power to enforce, by appropriate legislation, the provisions of this article.

---

### AMENDMENT XV

Section 1. The right of citizens of the United States to vote shall not be denied or abridged by the United States or by any State on account of race, color, or previous condition of servitude.

Section 2. The Congress shall have power to enforce this article by appropriate legislation.

### AMENDMENT XVI

The Congress shall have power to lay and collect taxes on incomes, from whatever source derived, without apportionment among the several States, and without regard to any census or enumeration.

### AMENDMENT XVII

The Senate of the United States shall be composed of two Senators from each State, elected by the people thereof, for six years; and each Senator shall have one vote. The electors in each State shall have the qualifications requisite for electors of the most numerous branch of the State legislatures.

When vacancies happen in the representation of any State in the Senate, the executive authority of such State shall issue writs of election to fill such vacancies: *Provided,* That the legislature of any State may empower the executive thereof to make temporary appointments until the people fill the vacancies by election as the legislature may direct.

This amendment shall not be so construed as to affect the election or term of any Senator chosen before it becomes valid as part of the Constitution.

### AMENDMENT XVIII

[Section 1. After one year from the ratification of this article the manufacture, sale, or transportation of intoxicating liquors within, the importation thereof into, or the exportation thereof from the United States and all territory subject to the jurisdiction thereof for beverage purposes is hereby prohibited.

[Sec. 2. The Congress and the several States shall have concurrent power to enforce this article by appropriate legislation.

[Sec. 3. This article shall be inoperative unless it shall have been ratified as an amendment to the Constitution by the legislatures of the several States, as provided in the Constitution, within seven years from the date of the submission hereof to the States by the Congress.]

197

AMENDMENT XIX

The right of citizens of the United States to vote shall not be denied or abridged by the United States or by any State on account of sex.

Congress shall have power to enforce this article by appropriate legislation.

AMENDMENT XX

Section 1. The terms of the President and Vice-President shall end at noon on the 20th day of January, and the terms of Senators and Representatives at noon on the 3d day of January, of the years in which such terms would have ended if this article had not been ratified; and the terms of their successors shall then begin.

Sec. 2. The Congress shall assemble at least once in every year, and such meeting shall begin at noon on the 3d day of January, unless they shall by law appoint a different day.

Sec. 3. If, at the time fixed for the beginning of the term of the President, the President elect shall have died, the Vice-President elect shall become President. If a President shall not have been chosen before the time fixed for the beginning of his term, or if the President elect shall have failed to qualify, then the Vice-President elect shall act as President until a President shall have qualified; and the Congress may by law provide for the case wherein neither a President elect nor a Vice-President elect shall have qualified, declaring who shall then act as President, or the manner in which one who is to act shall be selected, and such person shall act accordingly until a President or Vice-President shall have qualified.

Sec. 4. The Congress may by law provide for the case of the death of any of the persons from whom the House of Representatives may choose a President whenever the right of choice shall have devolved upon them, and for the case of the death of any of the persons from whom the Senate may choos a Vice-President whenever the right of choice shall have devolved upon them.

Sec. 5. Sections 1 and 2 shall take effect on the 15th day of October following the ratification of this article.

Sec. 6. This article shall be inoperative unless it shall have been ratified as an amendment to the Constitution by the legislatures of three-fourths of the several States within seven years from the date of its submission.

### AMENDMENT XXI

Section 1. The eighteenth article of amendment to the Constitution of the United States is hereby repealed.

Sec. 2. The transportation or importation into any State, Territory, or possession of the United States for delivery or use therein of intoxicating liquors, in violation of the laws thereof, is hereby prohibited.

Sec. 3. This article shall be inoperative unless it shall have been ratified as an amendment to the Constitution by conventions in the several States, as provided in the Constitution, within seven years from the date of the submission hereof to the States by the Congress.

### AMENDMENT XXII

Section 1. No person shall be elected to the office of the President more than twice, and no person who has held the office of President, or acted as President, for more than two years of a term to which some other person was elected President shall be elected to the office of the President more than once. But this Article shall not apply to any person holding the office of President when this Article was proposed by the Congress, and shall not prevent any person who may be holding the office of President, or acting as President, during the term within which this Article becomes operative from holding the office of President or acting as President during the remainder of such term.

Sec. 2. This article shall be inoperative unless it shall have been ratified as an amendment to the Constitution by the legislatures of three-fourths of the several States within seven years from the date of its submission to the States by the Congress.

### AMENDMENT XXIII

Section 1. The District constituting the seat of Government of the United States shall appoint in such manner as the Congress may direct:

A number of electors of President and Vice-President equal to the whole number of Senators and Representatives in Congress to which the District would be entitled if it were a State, but in no event more than the least populous State; they shall be in addition to those appointed by the States, but they shall be considered, for the purposes of the election of President and Vice-President, to be electors appointed by a

199

State; and they shall meet in the District and perform such duties as provided by the twelfth article of amendment.

Sec. 2. The Congress shall have power to enforce this article by appropriate legislation.

### AMENDMENT XXIV

Section 1. The right of citizens of the United States to vote in any primary or other election for President or Vice-President, for electors for President or Vice-President, or for Senator or Representative in Congress, shall not be denied or abridged by the United States or any State by reason of failure to pay any poll tax or other tax.

Sec. 2. The Congress shall have power to enforce this article by appropriate legislation.

### AMENDMENT XXV

Section 1. In case of removal of the President from office or of his death or resignation, the Vice-President shall become President.

Sec. 2. Whenever there is a vacancy in the office of the Vice-President, the President shall nominate a Vice-President who shall take office upon confirmation by a majority vote of both Houses of Congress.

Sec. 3. Whenever the President transmits to the President pro tempore of the Senate and the Speaker of the House of Representatives his written declaration that he is unable to discharge the powers and duties of his office, and until he transmits to them a written declaration to the contrary, such powers and duties shall be discharged by the Vice-President as Acting President.

Sec. 4. Whenever the Vice-President and a majority of either the principal officers of the executive departments or of such other body as Congress may by law provide, transmit to the President pro tempore of the Senate and the Speaker of the House of Representatives their written declaration that the President is unable to discharge the powers and duties of his office, the Vice-President shall immediately assume the powers and duties of the office as Acting President.

Thereafter, when the President transmits to the President pro tempore of the Senate and the Speaker of the House of Representatives his written declaration that no inability exists, he shall resume the powers and duties of his office unless the Vice-President and a majority of either the principal officers of the executive department or of such other body as Congress may by law, provide, transmit within four days to the President pro tempore of the Senate and the Speaker of the House of Representatives their written declaration that the President is unable to discharge the powers and duties of his office. Thereupon Congress shall decide the issue, assembling within forty-eight hours for that purpose if not in session. If the Congress, within twenty-one days after receipt of the latter written declaration, or, if Congress is not in session, within twenty-one days after Congress is required to assemble, determines by two-thirds vote of both Houses that the President is unable to discharge the powers and duties of his office, the Vice-President shall continue to discharge the same as Acting President; otherwise, the President shall resume the powers and duties of his office.

### AMENDMENT XXVI

Section 1. The right of citizens of the United States, who are eighteen years of age or older, to vote shall not be denied or abridged by the United States or by any State on account of age.

Sec. 2. The Congress shall have power to enforce this article by appropriate legislation.

# Selected Books
# for Further Reading

ALLEN, CARLETON K., *Democracy and the Individual.* New York, Oxford University Press, 1943.

BOWEN, CATHERINE DRINKER, *Miracle at Philadelphia.* Boston, Little, Brown, 1966.

BRANT, IRVING, *The Bill of Rights—Its Origin and Meaning.* Indianapolis, Bobbs-Merrill, 1965.

CHAFEE, ZECHARIAH, JR., *The Blessings of Liberty.* Philadelphia, Lippincott, 1956.

CLAUDE, RICHARD, *The Supreme Court and the Electoral Process.* Baltimore, Johns Hopkins Press, 1970.

DOUGLAS, WILLIAM O., *A Living Bill of Rights.* New York, Doubleday, 1961.

———, *We the Judges.* New York, Doubleday, 1956.

KONVITZ, MILTON V., *Bill of Rights Reader,* 2nd ed. Ithaca, New York, Cornell University Press, 1968.

LERNER, MAX, *America As a Civilization.* New York, Simon & Schuster, 1957.

MILLER, HELEN HILL, *The Case for Liberty.* Chapel Hill, University of North Carolina Press, 1965.

MORISON, SAMUEL ELIOT, and COMMAGER, HENRY STEELE, *The Growth of the American Republic.* New York, Oxford University Press, 1969.

WILLIAMS, EDWARD BENNETT, *One Man's Freedom.* New York, Atheneum, 1962.